How JavaScript Works

Master the Basics of JavaScript and Modern Web App Development

Jonathon Simpson

Apress®

How JavaScript Works: Master the Basics of JavaScript and Modern Web App Development

Jonathon Simpson
Belfast, Antrim, UK

ISBN-13 (pbk): 978-1-4842-9737-7
https://doi.org/10.1007/978-1-4842-9738-4

ISBN-13 (electronic): 978-1-4842-9738-4

Copyright © 2023 by Jonathon Simpson

Managing Director, Apress Media LLC: Welmoed Spahr
Acquisitions Editor: James Robinson-Prior
Development Editor: James Markham
Editorial Assistant: Gryffin Winkler

Cover designed by eStudioCalamar

Cover image designed by onlyyouqj on freepik

Distributed to the book trade worldwide by Springer Science+Business Media New York, 1 New York Plaza, Suite 4600, New York, NY 10004-1562, USA. Phone 1-800-SPRINGER, fax (201) 348-4505, e-mail orders-ny@springer-sbm.com, or visit www.springeronline.com. Apress Media, LLC is a California LLC and the sole member (owner) is Springer Science + Business Media Finance Inc (SSBM Finance Inc). SSBM Finance Inc is a **Delaware** corporation.

For information on translations, please e-mail booktranslations@springernature.com; for reprint, paperback, or audio rights, please e-mail bookpermissions@springernature.com.

Apress titles may be purchased in bulk for academic, corporate, or promotional use. eBook versions and licenses are also available for most titles. For more information, reference our Print and eBook Bulk Sales web page at http://www.apress.com/bulk-sales.

Any source code or other supplementary material referenced by the author in this book is available to readers on GitHub. For more detailed information, please visit https://www.apress.com/gp/services/source-code.

Paper in this product is recyclable

Table of Contents

About the Author

Jonathon Simpson studied at UCL and currently works in product development at Revolut, a global neobank and financial technology company that offers banking services. He has over 15 years of web development experience working on a wide range of products and services. Jonathon also owns and operates a popular software engineering blog focusing on JavaScript and web development.

About the Technical Reviewer

Russ Ferguson is a web application developer living in Brooklyn, New York. He has worked on projects for organizations such as Ann Taylor, MTV, DC Comics, and LG. Currently, he is the Vice President at Bank of America managing a team of Angular developers, building internal applications.

Introduction

JavaScript is one of the most used programming languages in the world. When JavaScript was first created, it was a useful tool for adding interactivity to web pages. Since then, it has evolved to power back-end servers, massive front-end web applications, and even iPhone and Android applications via tools like Electron and Tauri.

While JavaScript has matured as a language its complexity seems to have increased. What started as simple scripts inside HTML tags now seems to involve compile steps via TypeScript and frameworks like React, Vue.js, or Svelte. For those getting started in JavaScript, it can be overwhelming, even though these tools are just an additional level of abstraction which ultimately compiles down into vanilla JavaScript.

In this book, we'll learn how JavaScript works from the bottom up, which will prepare you for everything web development and JavaScript-led app development can throw at you. We'll also explain some of the quirks you'll find in JavaScript and how many of them have come to be due to JavaScript's long and varied history.

After that, we'll cover JavaScript's unique approach to inheritance before moving into more complicated topics like memory management, classes, APIs, and web workers. We'll explore how the weakly typed system JavaScript employs has both benefits and downsides.

As a fundamental part of the web stack, and with more people using it every day, there has never been a better time to learn JavaScript. This book will guide you through everything you need to know, so that you can master modern web app development.

CHAPTER 1

Introduction to JavaScript

JavaScript is a programming language that first appeared in 1995 as the scripting language for the Netscape browser. Since then, it has evolved into one of the most used programming languages in the world. While its initial goal was to add interactivity to websites, it has since come to do just about everything, including creating desktop apps and back-end APIs.

JavaScript is everywhere, and over the years, many frameworks have been built on top of it, such as jQuery, React, Vue.js, and Svelte. All of this can make learning JavaScript intimidating, as there are often many different ways to achieve the same thing.

In this book, we'll be covering how JavaScript works at a fundamental level. That will then make it is easier to understand how frameworks like React and Vue.js work. We'll discuss why things work the way they do in JavaScript and the various quirks that come with years of ongoing development on the language.

JavaScript today broadly falls into two major categories:

- **Client-side** code, which we'll refer to as "the front end," which is included via HTML files and adds interactivity to websites. Client-side code is loaded and processed directly on someone's web browser or device. In practice, this means writing a .js file or HTML file containing JavaScript and loading it directly into your web browser.

© Jonathon Simpson 2023
J. Simpson, *How JavaScript Works*, https://doi.org/10.1007/978-1-4842-9738-4_1

- **Server-side** code, which we'll refer to as "the back end," which is used for writing web servers. This kind of code is written on web servers and can be used to create things like APIs which the end user never directly sees. It uses a runtime to execute the code on web servers. The most common runtime used for this is called Node.js. Server side code is loaded and processed on a server that is separate from the user's device.

Everything we discuss in this book will be applicable to both front end and back end, but our focus will be on front-end JavaScript since that's where JavaScript started. We'll sometimes touch on back-end JavaScript where necessary so that certain concepts can be more easily understood.

JavaScript Fundamentals

JavaScript is based on a language standard called ECMAScript. How JavaScript should exactly work is documented in a specific standard called ECMA-262. Since ECMAScript does not provide any tools to compile JavaScript, every implementation of JavaScript creates its own version of JavaScript. That includes your browser and back-end compilers like Node.js.

For the most part, these implementations follow ECMA-262, but since each implementation is done by different teams, there can be some minor discrepancies or different feature sets depending on the browser or implementation.

In this chapter, we will be covering how you can set yourself up to start using JavaScript, including how to set up JavaScript projects when using Node.js. In future chapters, we will explore *how* to write JavaScript code.

JavaScript's Type Classification

How a language is typed usually gives us a broad idea of how it works. Like most other languages, JavaScript lets you define "variables" to store data, and these variables have types. "Type" refers to the kind of data being used. For example, a number is of type `Number`, and a mixture of characters and/or numbers is referred to as having a type called `String`.

If you have used other languages, JavaScript may seem different since it is **weakly typed**. That means that while other languages require you to explicitly mention in the code what type of data different variables are, JavaScript does not. JavaScript is also often referred to as **dynamically typed**, meaning it will dynamically interpret what type of data is based on the context it finds it in.

To understand this better, let's look at how variables are defined in JavaScript. Usually, we define them like this:

```
let x = "Some String"
let y = 5
let z = false
```

You'll see that no types are defined here. For example, we did not have to mention that `"Some String"` was a `String`. JavaScript determines types based on context – so it will take x to be a `String` simply because we put its value in quotation marks. Similarly, it will dynamically interpret y as being of type `Number` since it lacks quotation marks and z as being of type `Boolean` since it has no quotation marks and uses the keyword `false`.

This makes JavaScript quite easy to pick up, but quite hard to master. The lack of strong typing can mean that you unknowingly create bugs in your software since JavaScript will not always throw errors if unexpected types show up, and even worse, JavaScript may dynamically interpret types incorrectly in some cases.

For more complex applications with lots of test cases, developers often reach for **TypeScript** instead of JavaScript for this reason. TypeScript *is* JavaScript, but *extended*. It's strongly typed, meaning types must be mentioned in your code.

What Is JavaScript Used For?

As we mentioned in the introduction, JavaScript can be compiled and used in two major ways. The first is to create front-end interactive experiences, right in your browser. The second is as back-end server code. Front-end JavaScript is rendered by the browser inside of web pages, while back-end server code requires a runtime like Node.js, which compiles the code you write to run it directly on the server.

When inside the browser, some of the major things JavaScript can do are

- Adding, changing, or deleting CSS/HTML when a user interacts with something.

- Creating new HTML tags programmatically.

- Tracking user action and producing feedback to the user (such as showing a pop-up when a user clicks on something).

- Storing data for the user locally via local storage or cookies.

- Creating single-page user experiences where no page refreshing is needed.

On the back end, the main use cases are

- Creating routes/URL endpoints on a server and dictate what happens if a user navigates there.

- Creating routes/URL endpoints for APIs (application programming interfaces), so we can send and receive data to and from the server.

- Building WebSocket servers, which users can interact with from their front-end experience. These can be used for making things like chat rooms.

- Compressing pre-rendered web pages for a faster web experience.

- Manipulating data sent to the server (sometimes via WebSocket or API) and store it in a back-end database.

Writing JavaScript

JavaScript on the front end is found inside HTML on web pages. As such, familiarity with HTML is quite important when we work with JavaScript. To create your first file containing JavaScript, you can start by making a `.html` file. We usually call the home page of a website `index.html` when building websites, so for this example, I created a new HTML file called `index.html`.

`.html` files can be opened by any web browser, such as Google Chrome. You can edit your HTML file by opening it up in a text or code editor (Notepad included), and puting in this standard "boilerplate" HTML:

```
<!DOCTYPE html>
<html>
<head>
    <title>My First JavaScript</title>
</head>
<body>
<p>Hello World</p>
```

```
<script type="text/javascript">
    // This is JavaScript!
</script>
</body>
</html>
```

Note   You can use any text editor (like Notepad) to create HTML and even JavaScript. While that works fine, it's better to use a professional code editor instead. One of the most popular code editors used in the software development community is VS Code. You can download it via `https://code.visualstudio.com/`. This will color code your JavaScript and give you a lot of other useful features.

In the preceding example, we inserted a `<script>` tag within our HTML body. The `<script>` tag is where our JavaScript goes:

```
<script type="text/javascript">
    // This is JavaScript!
</script>
```

Since JavaScript applications can get quite long, you may see this `<script>` tag substituted out for a file instead. This can be useful since it lets us separate our HTML and JavaScript into different files.

For example, if we had a separate JavaScript file called `myScript.js` stored in the same folder as `index.html` file, we could load that into our HTML document by using the `src` attribute on the `script` tag:

```
<script src="myScript.js"></script>
```

You may also see JavaScript embedded into HTML via the attributes of HTML tags. For example, JavaScript can be put inside a button to cause something to happen when a user clicks that button:

```
<button onclick="//JavaScript here"></button>
```

Setting Up a Code Editor

Throughout this book, I will be writing code using Visual Studio Code or VS Code. If you do not have a preferred code editor, I would strongly recommend using VS Code, which you can download via the official website (https://code.visualstudio.com).

Although it is possible to build a software career through Notepad, it's not recommended. Modern code editors like VS Code give you a ton of useful features, including code highlighting which makes it easier to read what you're writing. They also come with more advanced features like built-in terminals, for when you need those things.

If you download VS Code, you'll be greeted with a screen that looks like the one shown in Figure 1-1. From there, you'll be able to make new files and folders for storing your projects in.

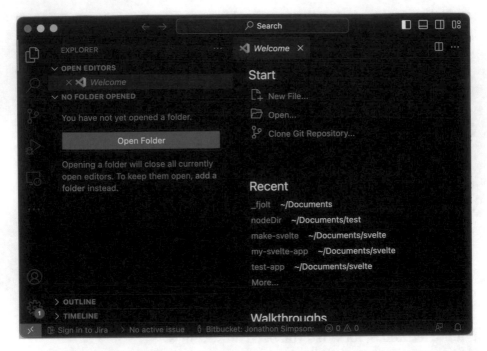

Figure 1-1. *After you install VS Code, open the application. By going to File ➤ Open Folder… or clicking "Open Folder" in VS Code and finding your "My JavaScript" folder*

Starting Up Our Code

The fun thing about writing front-end JavaScript is that once you save your .html file, you can load it directly in any web browser to test it out.

Try it out by opening index.html in your web browser, either by dragging it into the window or by opening it via File ➤ Open File….

To see your code in the browser itself, you can right-click on the web page anywhere and choose "Inspect" in Google Chrome. If Chrome is not your browser of choice, similar functions exist in other browsers too. Using "Inspect" will also let you see supplementary information about what you've created, as Figure 1-2 shows.

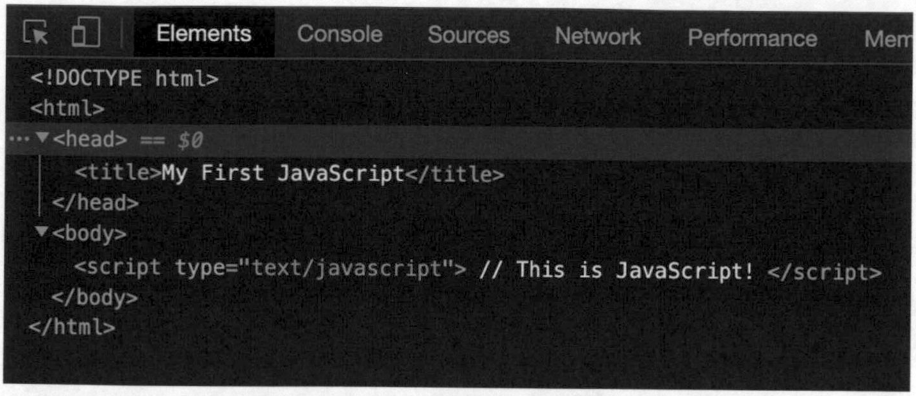

Figure 1-2. "Inspect" or "Inspect Element" lets you view more information about your code in the web browser

"Inspect" or "Inspect Element" is a vital tool in web development. Throughout this book, we'll use the console tab within developer tools to test out code and see the results of code we run. As such, it's very useful to familiarize yourself with this display now.

How to Get Started with Writing Back-End JavaScript

We've now discussed how JavaScript can be run inside a web browser like Google Chrome. Before we go any further, let's briefly look at how we run back-end JavaScript too, which we'll occasionally touch on in this book. Back end JavaScript runs directly on your computer or a web server instead of inside a web browser. To run JavaScript like this, you need to use a runtime like Node.js.

Node.js can be downloaded and installed on your computer via the official Node.js website (https://nodejs.org/en/download). After it has been installed, you'll be able to run JavaScript code directly from a terminal window by executing your .js file.

You can do that by opening the terminal or command line on your computer, which is accessible on MacOS via the terminal app or on Windows via the "cmd" application.

Running the node command lets you compile and execute JavaScript files. **Let's try it out** – create a file called index.js in a code editor or Notepad, and add the following JavaScript code before saving:

```
console.log("Hello World!")
```

Then you can execute this file by using the node command in terminal:

```
node index.js
```

This will produce an output which looks something like what is shown in Figure 1-3.

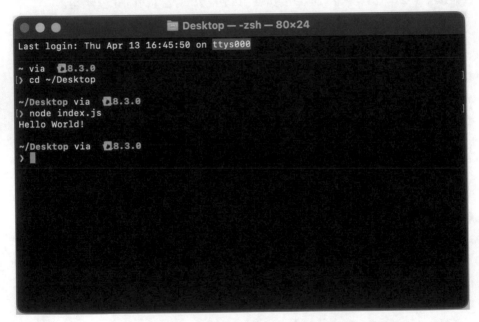

Figure 1-3.   Running a JavaScript script from the command line is as simple as using the "node" command followed by the directory link to the file you want to run

Note   If you saved your index.js file in another directory, you will need to provide the full directory link. To navigate directories, use the `cd` command. For example, if your index.js file was in "/Users/JohnDoe/Documents/", you would run `cd /Users/JohnDoe/Documents/` and only after that, run node `index.js`.

Node.js applications like this are frequently used to create APIs, which we will cover in much more detail later in the book.

Creating Node.js JavaScript Projects

In the above example, we executed a single file using Node.js It is more common, though, to create a Node.js project when you start something new in Node.js. This is also done via terminal or the cmd. The first step is to make a new folder and navigate to it using the `cd` command.

In this example, I made a folder called "node-project" on my desktop and navigated to it using the following command in Terminal:

```
cd ~/Desktop/node-project
```

After that's done, you can use the `npm init` command, which is installed along with Node.js, to initiate your project. You can see how that looks in Figure 1-4.

```
● ● ●  ■  My Node Project — npm init __CFBundleIdentifier=com.apple.Terminal T...
Last login: Thu Apr 13 17:23:11 on ttys000

~ via  □8.3.0
|> cd ~/Desktop/"My Node Project"

~/Desktop/My Node Project
|> npm init
This utility will walk you through creating a package.json file.
It only covers the most common items, and tries to guess sensible defaults.

See `npm help init` for definitive documentation on these fields
and exactly what they do.

Use `npm install <pkg>` afterwards to install a package and
save it as a dependency in the package.json file.

Press ^C at any time to quit.
package name: (my-node-project) █
```

Figure 1-4. *When using the npm init command, you will be asked to enter some information about your new project as shown earlier*

All you have to do now is type in answers to each question and press enter. For example, the first question asks what you want to call your project – so type in the name of your project, and press enter.

Your folder will now contain a package.json file summarizing the information you provided. Since you've initialized your Node.js project, you'll now be able to run other commands like npm install now, which lets you install third party dependencies.

JavaScript Support

Traditional software is usually written by a developer and downloaded onto a user's computer or device. This is the case with things like video games, apps on your phone, or big applications like Adobe Photoshop.

When writing code in JavaScript, things are very different. The software the user installs is the browser, not your website! The browser then loads your web page within it. Since everyone has their own browser preference, and not everyone keeps their browsers up to date, JavaScript that works in one browser can oftentimes not work in another. For example, Firefox may support a new JavaScript feature, but Chrome may not. The worst thing about this is you can't really use a new JavaScript feature on the front end until a majority of browsers have implemented it.

If you are coming from other languages, then worrying about browser support will be a foreign concept to you. In JavaScript, it is a *real* thing. In recent times, since most browsers are "evergreen" (meaning they auto-update), this has become less of a problem than it used to be, but sometimes different browsers just disagree on what should and shouldn't be implemented. Promising new features may end up implemented in just Chrome, just Safari, or just Firefox.

Throughout this book, we'll only be looking at JavaScript with broad browser support, meaning you don't need to worry about if you can or can't use it. However, when you start exploring JavaScript in your own time, and especially when looking at more advanced functionality, it's important to check if browsers support it. You can find good browser support tables on websites like `https://caniuse.com/` or `https://developer.mozilla.org/`.

An example of a browser support table can be found in Figure 1-5, for the GPU feature.

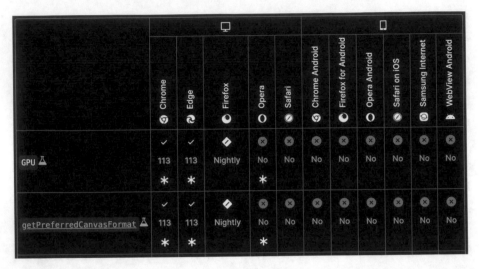

Figure 1-5. Not all browsers support every new JavaScript feature. In the preceding example, only Chrome and Edge have support. Other browsers only have partial support or none at all. That means if you tried to implement this on a website, only some users could use it!

Summary

In this chapter, we've looked at how to set up your workspace to begin writing code with JavaScript. We've discussed what JavaScript is typically used for and some of the pitfalls or differences between it and other languages. Now that we've covered the basics let's look at how to write JavaScript code.

CHAPTER 2

Code Structure and Logical Statements

In the previous chapter, we covered the fundamental definitions of JavaScript and where we write it. Now that we've discussed the basics, let's start learning about how we write JavaScript code. In this chapter, we'll cover the fundamentals, which includes code structure, logical statements, and variables. Mastering these concepts is a requirement to writing useful JavaScript code. Where relevant, we'll also be diving deeper into how these basic concepts actually work, so that you have a deeper understanding of the code you are writing.

Getting Started

As we go through this chapter, it will be good to have a work space where you can write and test your JavaScript. For these purposes, I've created a folder called "javascript-project" in my documents folder. Within that, I have created two files – index.html and index.js.

Since our focus will be writing JavaScript, your HTML file can be relatively simple:

```html
<!DOCTYPE html>
<html>
    <head>
        <title>My First JavaScript</title>
    </head>
```

© Jonathon Simpson 2023
J. Simpson, *How JavaScript Works*, https://doi.org/10.1007/978-1-4842-9738-4_2

```
    <body>
        <p>Hello World</p>
        <script src="index.js"></script>
    </body>
</html>
```

Any JavaScript code you want to try out can be put in index.js. For now, I've only put a simple console.log method:

```
console.log("Hello World!")
```

The console.log method is really useful. It's used extensively for debugging, and we'll be using it throughout this book. When it's run, it logs a message to your browser's console, so that you can see the output of your code easily. You can find the console by right-clicking anywhere on your web page and selecting "Inspect." Console logs can then be viewed under the "Console" tab, as shown in Figure 2-1.

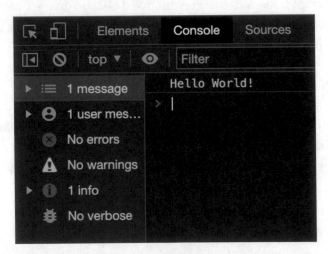

Figure 2-1. Right-clicking in the web browser and selecting "Inspect" in Google Chrome (or other browsers) allows you to access the console log. If you do this with the index.html file we defined before, you'll see "Hello World!" written here. The console is a powerful tool used for debugging. When we use the console.log method, it shows up here!

Common Code Conventions

Before we start writing real code, let's first consider some basic code conventions. As is the case in most programming, developers of JavaScript try to follow some common conventions when writing code. This section is largely opinionated, but it does provide you with guidelines on how you should go about writing JavaScript. It will also let you know how we will go about writing code throughout the book.

Semicolons

For readability, JavaScript is sometimes written with a semicolon at the end of each line. For example:

```
console.log("Hello World!");
console.log("Goodbye World!");
```

However, this is not necessary, and it's also just as common to see the same code written without semicolons:

```
console.log("Hello World!")
console.log("Goodbye World!")
```

We can do this because JavaScript will intuitively "figure out" where semicolons should go. It even works if you do an accidental line break where an expression seems incomplete. For example, if a line ends with a + symbol, JavaScript will assume that the expression must continue onto the next line, meaning the code will still work as expected:

```
console.log(5 +
6)
```

For the code in this book, we will be omitting the semicolon unless it is really needed.

Spacing

One of the most vigorously fought over code conventions is whether to use tabs or spaces for indenting. While there is essentially no right or wrong answer to this, it is important to be *consistent*. If you use tabs, then always use tabs for indents and likewise for spaces.

Unlike Python, indents play no functional role in JavaScript, but they do serve to make your code more readable when others look at it. While it is certainly fine to use tabs, spaces are going to cause you less of a headache. That's because different ecosystems and operating systems can be configured to handle tabs differently, whereas spaces are consistently sized across all systems.

In this book, we will indent with four spaces. Here is an example of how that will look:

```
let myVariable = 5

if(myVariable === 5) {
    console.log("The variable is 5!")
}
```

Note   If you use the tab key instead of spaces in VS Code to indent your code, you can configure VS Code to automatically convert these to spaces if you want it to. The configuration option is found by opening any file and selecting the "Spaces/Tab Size" option in the bottom right-hand corner.

Variable and Function Naming

When it comes to naming functions and variables, you'll come across three different paradigms: camel case, pascal case, and underscores:

- Camel case refers to naming a variable where every word after the first has a capital letter, for example, `thisIsCamelCase`.

- Pascal case is the same, except the first letter is capitalized too. For example, `ThisIsPasalCase`.

- Underscoring refers to separating words with underscores. For example, `these_are_underscored`.

When naming variables and functions, all of these are fine to use, but again, it is important to be consistent. If you decide to use camel case, then make sure you use it everywhere. For the purposes of this book, we will be using camel case.

JavaScript Variables

As we begin writing JavaScript, the first thing you're going to need to learn about are variables. Variables are a way to assign a fixed name to a data value. There are three ways to create a variable in JavaScript, using three different keywords:

- `var`
- `let`
- `const`

All JavaScript variables are case-sensitive, so `myVariable` is different from `MYVARIABLE`. In JavaScript nomenclature, we usually say that we "declare" variables.

Setting Variables with let

Most variables in JavaScript are set with let. A variable set with let starts with the keyword let, followed by the variable name and an equals sign, and then the value of your variable. In the following example, we create a variable called myVariable, and console log it so that it appears in the browser's console:

```
let myVariable = 5
console.log(myVariable)
```

Note   It may seem like we are putting data into the variable, but a better way to think about it is we are making data and then pointing the keyword "myVariable" at the data we just made.

It's not possible to assign a variable with let twice. If you think of your variable as pointing to some data, it's easy to see why – the same variable can't point to two different pieces of data. For example, the following code will produce the error, which is shown in Figure 2-2.

```
let myVariable = 5
let myVariable = 10
console.log(myVariable)
```

Figure 2-2. *Variables defined with let cannot be defined multiple times. If you try to, it will produce an error like the preceding one*

So variables defined with `let` cannot be redefined again. They can, however, be reassigned to a new piece of data by mentioning them again without the `let` keyword. You can see that in the following example, which console logs "10," since we changed the value of `myVariable`:

```
let myVariable = 5
myVariable = 10
console.log(myVariable)
```

It may seem like the data has changed (or "mutated"), but actually we've just made new data somewhere and pointed our variable to that instead. The data "5" still exists somewhere. It just has no variable pointing to it anymore. When a piece of data is no longer referenced in our code, JavaScript may remove it from memory using something called "garbage collection." This allows JavaScript to free up memory when data is no longer used.

Block Scoping with Variables

In the previous example we saw that it is not possible to define the same variable, but there are exceptions to this. That's because variables defined with `let` are block-scoped. Scope confines functionality, variable names, and values to certain sections of our code.

Block scopes are created with curly brackets {}. In most scenarios, we create block scopes by defining new functions or logical statements.

Since standalone curly brackets also create a new block scope, a variable can be set twice simply by defining it again inside { } curly brackets:

```
let myVariable = 5

{
    let myVariable = 10
    console.log(myVariable)
}

console.log(myVariable)
```

Even though we created the same variable twice, no error is thrown, and that's because one is assigned to a new block scope. The first variable is assigned to the "global" scope of our program, while the second is assigned only to the "curly bracket" scope. The outcome of this can be seen in Figure 2-3.

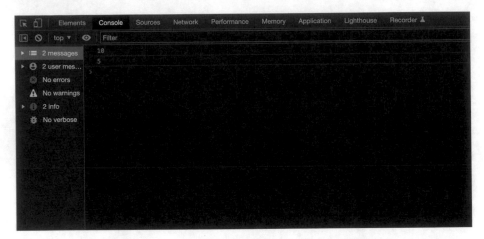

Figure 2-3. *While using* `let`*, our console produces two different lines, 5 and 10. This is because let is assigned to its current scope – so setting* `myVariable` *to 10 in a separate scope does not affect the original variable. If we used* `var` *instead, both lines would say 10 since scope is ignored*

Setting Variables with var

Most variables are set with `let`, but you may also see the keyword `var` being used to set variables sometimes. Using `var` is the original way to set variables in JavaScript. It is valuable to know this exists, but it is generally not recommended that you use it over `let`.

Setting a variable with `var` looks a lot like what we did with `let`. For example, here is a variable called `myVariable`, with a value of 5:

```
var myVariable = 5
```

The reason why we use `let` rather than `var` is because `var` has a few quirks that `let` does not. For example, you can define a variable twice with `var`, and no errors will be thrown:

```
var myVariable = 5
var myVariable = 10
console.log(myVariable)
```

Variables defined with `var` are also not block-scoped, meaning your code can produce some odd results when redefining variables in block scopes with `var`.

You may be wondering, "Why does JavaScript have two ways of defining variables when `let` is a more controlled version of `var`?" The answer to that is pretty simple, and it's because `var` used to be the only way to define variables in JavaScript, and a lot of legacy code uses it. Later on, JavaScript created a better way to define variables using `let`, but `var` couldn't be removed since it would break many older code bases.

Setting Variables with const

The final variable type we will cover is `const`. When we defined variables with `let`, we talked about how a variable can be reassigned to another value:

```
let myVariable = 5
myVariable = 10
console.log(myVariable)
```

Remember, we don't actually change or "mutate" the data here – we just create new data and "re-point" our variable to that new data source.

While this works for `let`, it will not work for `const`. Variables defined with `const` are constants and cannot be reassigned:

```
const myConst = 5
console.log(myConst)
```

If you try to reassign the value of a `const` variable, you'll get an error instead.

❌ `const myConst = 5`

```
myConst = 10
console.log(myConst)
```

Using `const` to define variables is better when you're able to use it. To understand why, you can think about the example we discussed earlier where we used `let` to reassign a variable from "5" to "10". We talked about how the value "5" still exists in memory unless it gets garbage collected. Since `const` variables cannot be changed, garbage collection never has to run. That means less cleanup is required, resulting in more efficient memory utilisation.

Mutation of const Variables

Variables cannot be reassigned with `const`, but they can be mutated. That's because reassignment and mutation are not the same thing. When we reassign a variable, no data changes – but it is possible to change underlying data in JavaScript using mutation instead. In JavaScript, mutation of primitive values like numbers, strings, and booleans is not possible, but objects can be mutated.

We will cover how arrays and objects work in more depth in the next chapter. For now, all you need to understand is that arrays and objects are containers of data. An array can be defined as shown in the following example:

```
const myArray = [ "some", "set", "of", "content" ]
console.log(myArray)
```

Arrays can contain a lot of data, and we can push new data to an array using a special method called push:

```
const myArray = [ "some", "set", "of", "content" ]
myArray.push("new data!")
console.log(myArray)
```

By using push we can mutate our array, meaning the underlying data changes and the data continues to be referenced and stored in the same place. In other words, we did not create new data and point our variable somewhere else, but instead mutated the original data.

This is confusing to beginners since the array was pointed to by a const variable, so it would therefore be assumed that since the const variable is a constant, the data inside must always remain constant. This is not the case in JavaScript. So, in summary, while reassignment must remain constant in a const variable, data mutation is fine.

Defining Variables Without Values

It is also possible to define variables that point to nowhere. If you try to console log a variable with no value assigned, you will get undefined as a result:

```
let myVariable
console.log(myVariable)
```

This is sometimes done when a variable does not have a value when you declare it but may be assigned a value later on in the code. When many variables need to be declared without values, they can be separated by commas. In the following example, we define three variables with the let keyword:

```
let myVariable, myOtherVariable, myFinalVariable
```

Although comma notation like this is more commonly used with variables that have no value, you can declare variables with values this way too:

```
let myVariable = 5, myOtherVariable = 4, myFinalVariable = 3
```

Assignment Operators

Now that we've covered the basics of setting variables, let's look at assignment operators. These allow us to modify an existing variable, by changing its value. For example, consider this variable:

```
let x = 5
```

Suppose we wanted to multiply x by 5. One way is to reassign x to 5 * 5, but a better way is to use an assignment operation. The reason it's better is because x may not always be 5, so this is particularly useful if we want to change the value of variables based on conditions (which we will cover in more detail in the following).

To multiply x by 5, we use the *= assignment operator:

```
let x = 5
x *= 5
console.log(x) // Console logs 25 (5 multiplied by 5 = 25)
```

There are many other assignment operators. They are shown in the following example:

```
let x = 5
x *= 5
console.log(x) // Console logs 25 (5 multiplied by 5 = 25)

x += 5
console.log(x) // Console logs 30 (25 plus 5 = 30)
```

```
x /= 5
console.log(x) // Console logs 6 (30 divided by 5 = 6)

x -= 1
console.log(x) // Console logs 5 (6 minus 1 = 5)

x %= 4
console.log(x)
/*
    Console logs 1 (if you divide 5 by 4, the remainder is 1.
    % is the remainder operator
*/
```

Variable Concatenation

When we have variables that consist of at least one string, using the +
operator causes the strings to become concatenated. To understand this,
take a look at the following example, where we concatenate two strings
into a new variable:

```
let myVariable = "hello"
let myOtherVariable = "world"
let combine = myVariable + myOtherVariable // "helloworld"
```

If we need a space too – we can add that with another +:

```
let myVariable = "hello"
let myOtherVariable = "world"

// "hello world"
let combine = myVariable + " " + myOtherVariable
```

Just be careful, since if you try to use a + with numbers, it will add them up instead!

```
let myVariable = 5
let myOtherVariable = 5

let combine = myVariable + myOtherVariable // 10
```

This brings us to a new quirk caused by JavaScript's dynamic typing. If a number is in quotation marks, it is assumed to be a string. Adding a number and string results in a new concatenated string instead of a calculation:

```
let myVariable = "5"
let myOtherVariable = 5

let combine = myVariable + myOtherVariable // "55"
```

Another way to combine string variables is with a special method called concat. This is a method that exists on all strings, which will add to the end of a string any number of new things that we separate with commas:

```
let myVariable = "hello"
myVariable.concat(" ", "world", "!") // hello world!
```

Different types of data have different built-in methods, which we'll look at in much more detail in future chapters.

Template Literals

Another final way to concatenate more elegantly is through a type of functionality called template literals. Template literals are still strings, but they use the backtick "`" to transform any content into a template literal. Template literals have the added benefit of allowing line breaks – something that numbers and quotation marks do not. They also allow for substitution. Here is an example of a particularly messy template literal with line breaks throughout:

```
let myVariable = `hello      world
    !!
how are     you?`
```

Template literals like the preceding one will be taken with line breaks and white space included – which means you'll avoid loss of this content when using them. They also allow for substitution. Adding a variable in ${} will substitute it into a template literal:

```
let someWord = "world"
let myVariable = `hello ${someWord}!` // hello world!
```

JavaScript Comments

You may have already noticed that in the preceding code, I used double slashes to leave some comments on what the code does. As our code gets more complicated, it's useful to leave messages to yourself or other developers about what is going on. For this purpose, comments are used.

A comment in JavaScript can take one of two forms. The first looks like this:

```
// I am a comment!
```

And the second looks like this, where the comment is enclosed in /* and */:

```
/* I am a comment! */
```

Both work the same, but the second allows for multiline comments. Comments have no bearing on the functionality of your code and instead can provide useful information on what's going on. For example, we could comment our previous code like so:

```
// This code will console log myConst
const myConst = 5
console.log(myConst)
```

Logical Statements

Now that we've covered variables, you'll probably be wondering how we can use them. Logical statements are one of the ways we can start to put our variables to good use.

Logical statements are used when we want to check if something is true or false and then run a particular action based on that outcome. If a logical statement is found to be `true`, everything within its "block scope" is executed. Likewise, if a logical statement is false, then the block scope will never run at all. In other words, logical statements allow us to build conditionality into our programs.

If...else Statements

`if...else` are perhaps one of the most commonly used logical statements around. All they do is check if a statement is true. If it is, they run some code, `else`, they run some other code. In the following example, we check if `myVariable` is set to 5. If it is, we show "The variable is 5!" in the console. If it's not, then we show alternative text.

You can view this code running in Figure 2-4, where I run it directly from the console in my web browser. You could also try this out by updating your index.js file from earlier:

```
// We have set myVariable to 5
let myVariable = 5

if(myVariable === 5) {
    console.log("The variable is 5!")
}
else {
    console.log("The variable is not 5.")
}
```

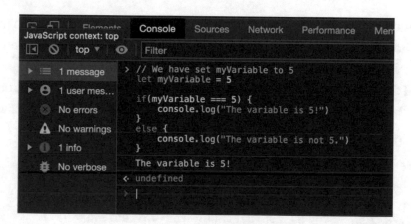

Figure 2-4. *Since myVariable is 5, the statement myVariable ===
5 is always true. So the block of code within the first if statement is
executed, and the else statement never fires*

We can add more conditions to our code by using else if after an if statement. In the following example, we check for a third condition, where myVariable could be 6:

```
// We have set myVariable to 5
let myVariable = 5

if(myVariable === 5) {
      console.log("The variable is 5!")
}
else if(myVariable === 6) {
      myVariable = 7
      console.log("The variable is 6, but I set it to 7!")
}
else {
      console.log("The variable is not 5.")
}
```

As you can see in the else if condition, any code can be written in the block scope created by a logical statement. In else if, we reassigned myVariable to have a value of 7.

If the output of an if statement is one line of code, you can omit the curly brackets and write it all on one line of code as shown in the following example. This also applies to else if and else:

```
// We have set myVariable to 5
let myVariable = 5

if(myVariable === 5) console.log("The variable is 5!")
```

Our examples so far have dealt with strict equality – meaning we are using the triple equals sign. There are more ways we can check variable values, though! We'll cover them all in this chapter.

Switch Statements

Another common way to create conditionality in your JavaScript is through switch statements. They take a single variable and check if it equals certain values using the case keyword to define the value it might equal and a break to declare the end of that clause. **For example:**

```
// Let's set x to 5
let x = 5

switch(x) {
    case 5:
        console.log("hello")
        break
    case 6:
        console.log("goodbye")
        break
}
```

In the previous example, we have two clauses: one where x equals 5, in which case we console log "hello," and another where it equals 6, where we console log "goodbye." It is important to have a break after each case clause since if you don't, all cases will run after the one that is correct! For example, the following code will console log both "hello" and "goodbye" – which is quite confusing:

```
// Let's set x to 5
let x = 5

switch(x) {
    case 4:
        console.log("4!")
    case 5:
        console.log("hello")
```

```
    case 6:
        console.log("goodbye")
}
```

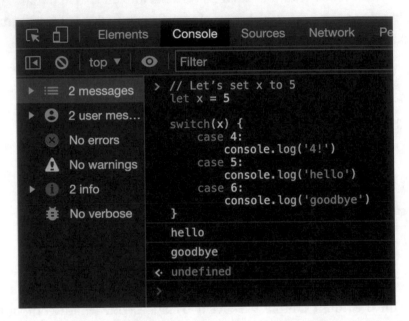

Figure 2-5. *Since we didn't use the keyword "break" in the preceding code and x is equal to 5, both "hello" and "goodbye" are console logged. The "break" keyword is important for declaring the end of a clause in a switch statement.*

This "fall-through" mechanism where we leave out a `break` statement can sometimes be used to your advantage, however. In the following example, both Apples and Strawberries are red, so console logging the same thing for both is not really an issue:

```
let x = "Apples"

switch(x) {
    case "Apples":
    case "Strawberries":
```

```
        console.log("Apples and Strawberries can be red.")
        break
    case "Bananas":
        console.log("Bananas are yellow.")
}
```

Defaulting to a Clause with Switch Statements

Switch statements make use of the keyword default to declare what needs to happen if none of the cases are matched. In the following example, the console will show "goodbye" since no clause is correct:

```
// Let's set x to 5
let x = 5

switch(x) {
    case 4: {
        console.log("hello")
        break
    }
    default: {
        console.log("goodbye")
        break
    }
}
```

Equality with Switch Statements

Like our example before with if…else, switch statements require "strict" equality. That means under the hood, they are using the triple equals sign (===). Strict equality means that both the value and type of the data must match for a clause to be true. This can sometimes be confusing in JavaScript since types are inferred. In the following example, both 5 and

"5" have the same value but different types. As such, only "goodbye" is shown in the console:

```
// Let's set x to 5
let x = 5

switch(x) {
    case "5": {
        console.log("hello")
        break
    }
    case 5: {
        console.log("goodbye")
        break
    }
}
```

Block Scoping with Logical Statements

Earlier, we discussed how block scopes affect let and const variables. Standard if...else statements by default have block scopes; as they use curly brackets {}, switch statements do not, by themselves, create block scopes. We can add block scope to our switch statements by enclosing each clause in curly brackets if we need to.

The outcome of the following code is an error since we reassign x multiple times: Uncaught SyntaxError: Identifier 'x' has already been declared:

```
// Let's set x to 5
let x = 5

switch(x) {
    case 5:
        let x = 6
        console.log("hello")
        break
    case 6:
        let x = 5
        console.log("goodbye")
        break
}
```

To avoid this error, a block scope can be created by adding curly brackets {} to our switch statement:

```
// Let's set x to 5
let x = 5

switch(x) {
    case 5: {
        let x = 6
        console.log("hello")
        break
    }
    case 6: {
        let x = 5
        console.log("goodbye")
        break
    }
}
```

Conditional Operator in Variables

So far we've covered statements that convey conditionality, but conditionality can also be extended to variable declarations themselves. This is done via a special operator called the conditional operator.

You can test any statement inside a variable by following it with a question mark. This is then followed by two values separated by a colon. The first value after the question mark will be what shows if the statement is true, and the second will be returned if the statement is false. In the following example, y becomes "Big Number" since x is indeed bigger than 3:

```
let x = 5

// Returns "Big Number"
let y = x > 3 ? "Big Number" : "Small Number"
```

Logical Statement Comparison Operators

In our previous examples, we've covered basic logical statements using strict equality (===). For example, if...else statements:

```
if(myVariable === 5)
```

and switch statements, which always use strict equality.:

```
switch(variable)
```

That means both the value and the type of data have to match for the statement to be true. For example, '5' is not the same type as 5 even though the values are the same since the types are different:

```
let myVariable = 5
if(myVariable === 5) // True!
if(myVariable === "5") // False!
```

Besides strict equality, there are lots of other ways we can compare data in logical statements. In the following example, we use the more than operator to check if myVariable is more than specific values. The outcome of this code can be seen in Figure 2-6.

```
let myVariable = 5
if(myVariable > 4) console.log("Hello World") // True!
if(myVariable > 6) console.log("Hello World 2!") // False!
```

Figure 2-6. *Other operators can be used to test logical statements. In the preceding example, we use the more than operator to check if* myVariable *meets certain conditions*

We can check for "regular" equality too, which ignores type, using the double equals (==) operator:

```
let myVariable = 5
if(myVariable == '5') // True!
```

The symbols we use to compare data in logical statements are generally known as "operators." All the operators we have access to are summarized in Table 2-1.

Table 2-1. *JavaScript operators for logical comparisons*

Operators	Definition	Example	
===	Strict equality. Both the type and value of the data must be the same.	5 === 5	// True
		5 === '5'	// False
==	Regular equality. Only the value must be the same.	5 == 5	// True
		5 == '5'	// True
>	More than. The value on the left must be more than the right.	6 > 5	// True
		5 > 5	// False
		4 > 5	// False
>=	More than or equal to. The value on the left must be more than or equal to the one on the right.	6 >= 5	// True
		5 >= 5	// True
		4 >= 5	// False
<	Less than. The value on the left must be less than the one on the right.	6 < 5	// False
		5 < 5	// False
		4 < 5	// True
<=	Less than or equal to. The value on the left must be less than or equal to the one on the right.	6 <= 5	// False
		5 <= 5	// True
		4 <= 5	// True
!==	Strict not equal to. The two values should not match value and type.	5 !== 5	// False
		5 !== '5'	// True
		5 !== 4	// True
!=	Regular not equal to. The two values should not match value.	5 !== 5	// False
		5 !== '5'	// False
		5 !== 4	// True

Logical Statement Logical Operators

Sometimes your logical statements may require that more than one statement is true. For example, checking if something is more than something **AND** less than something else. Three additional logical operators exist to combine statements, which can be found in Table 2-2.

Table 2-2. *JavaScript logical operators*

Operators	Definition
&&	AND – something AND something else is true.
||	OR – something OR something else is true.
!	NOT – something is NOT true.

In the following example, I am checking if a variable x is more than 5, but also less than or equal to 10 using the && AND operator:

```
let x = 6
if(x > 5 && x <= 10) {
    console.log('Hello World!')
}
```

Meanwhile, in this example, we check if x is more than 5 OR more than 3, using the || OR operator:

```
let x = 6
if(x > 5 || x > 3) {
    console.log('Hello World!')
}
```

We can also use the NOT operator to let us invert a result. For example, in the following we check if x is NOT more than 5 (by inverting x > 5):

```
let x = 6
if(!(x > 5)) {
    console.log('Hello World!')
}
```

Summary

In this chapter, we've covered some of the most important fundamental concepts of JavaScript. This has included some of the best practices for writing your code. We've also looked at how you can use variables to point to data and the difference between mutating data versus reassigning it. We've learned how to update those variables via assignment operators and how they can be used in a variety of logical statements. We have also discussed comments and how to add them to your code. All of these concepts are really important and required for the following chapters. As such, having a good grasp on this is critical to writing more complicated JavaScript.

CHAPTER 3

Introduction to Objects, Arrays

Now that we've now looked at the fundamental concepts of JavaScript, let's move onto one of the most important data types in JavaScript, that being objects. Objects are widely used in JavaScript as a store of data. They differ from other types of data in that they are the only type of data which is mutable.

In this chapter, we'll be covering the basics of how objects work. We'll also be covering arrays, which are a special type of object with specific features. As we get more comfortable with objects and arrays, we'll look at some more complicated concepts such as prototype-based programming and object inheritability.

Arrays

To start this chapter, let's look at arrays. Arrays are a special type of object which are used to store one-dimensional data. They have no explicitly defined keys. Arrays are usually defined inside [ ] square brackets which is different from objects, which we'll cover in more detail later, since they use { } curly brackets. In the following example, we create an array that contains a mixture of different types of data, including an object:

```
let myArr = [ "one", 2, "three", { "value": "four" } ]
```

J. Simpson, *How JavaScript Works*, https://doi.org/10.1007/978-1-4842-9738-4_3

The preceding square bracket notation we used is a type of "syntactic sugar." Syntactic sugar is another name for a cleaner and nicer way of writing something which we have to write all the time. Underneath the square brackets is a "constructor" called array. The previous example can be rewritten this way using the Array constructor:

```
let myArr = new Array("one", 2, "three", { "value": "four" })
```

The new keyword tells JavaScript to create a new instance of an object. That's also what the square brackets short hand does too. Since we create arrays all the time in JavaScript, it's much more common to use the square bracket [ ] notation. The square bracket notation is formally named the "**array literal**."

An array can contain any type of data – even things like functions. While arrays do not have explicitly defined keys, they do have numbered indices. Each array is zero-indexed – so to access the first item, we use the key is 0, and the second is 1, and others. To access specific array elements, we use square brackets again. The following example shows you how that works:

```
let myArr = [ "banana", "apple", "squid", "cake", "pear" ]
console.log(myArr[0]) // shows "banana"
console.log(myArr[2]) // shows "apple"
console.log(myArr[3]) // shows "squid"
```

Getting the Length of an Array

When we asked JavaScript to create a new instance of an Array, it also caused the array to inherit many standard methods and properties. All of these methods and properties have specific utilities.

One example of these is the length property, which is used to get the size of an array. Methods and properties on arrays can be accessed by using a dot, followed by that property or method's name. For example, to get the size of a given array, we use the .length method directly on that array.

Let's try putting the length of myArray into a new variable called arrayLength. When we console log this, it'll show 4:

```
let myArr = [ "one", 2, "three", { "value": "four" } ]
let arrayLength = myArr.length
console.log(arrayLength) // shows 4
```

Getting the Last Element of an Array

Knowing the length of an array is frequently used in the process of getting the last element of an array. Since arrays are zero-indexed, a common way to get the last element of an array is by using the .length method with 1 subtracted from it. The reason we subtract 1 is because if you start counting from zero, the last element's index is always going to be 1 less than the size of the array:

```
let myArr = [ "one", 2, "three", "four" ]
let arrayLength = myArr.length

console.log(myArr[myArr.length - 1]) // shows "four"
```

The array length here is 4, so subtracting 1 from that number results in 3, which is the index of the last element in the array.

While you will see this way of getting the last element of an array everywhere, a more modern and efficient method is to use the array method, .at(). Again, like length, .at() is predefined on all arrays.

Note on constructor methods   All arrays inherit a standard set of methods, which can be useful for performing common functions. Similarly, all other main types have constructor methods too – like strings, numbers, booleans, and objects.

The `.at()` method works a lot like retrieving an array element with square brackets. The main difference is that if you use negative numbers, it starts counting from the opposite end – so `.at(-1)` also gets the last element of an array:

```
let myArr = [ "one", 2, "three", "four" ]
let arrayLength = myArr.length

console.log(myArr.at(-1)) // shows "four"
```

Note   Square brackets are a standard notation in JavaScript arrays, but `at()` is a function. We haven't covered functions yet in detail, but functions can take arguments. In this case, `-1` is the argument we have used.

Array Manipulation Methods

We've now looked at how we can construct and create arrays, but in JavaScript development, it's common to also want to mutate or change arrays. To learn how this works, let's look at some methods that come in particularly useful when using arrays. Since objects (and therefore arrays) are mutable, many of these methods change the array value itself.

Push and Unshift

When we want to add an item to an array, push and unshift let us do that at the end and the start of the array, respectively. Adding items to the end of an array is always faster. The reason it is faster is because unshift needs to reallocate memory to add elements to the beginning of the array.

In the following example, push is used to add an item to the end of any array:

```
let myArr = [ "banana", "apple", "squid", "cake", "pear" ]
myArr.push("pear")
console.log(myArr) // [ "banana", "apple", "squid", "cake",
"pear" ]
```

In the next example, unshift is used to add something the beginning:

```
let myArr = [ "banana", "apple", "squid", "cake", "pear" ]
myArr.unshift("pear")
console.log(myArr) // [ "pear", "banana", "apple", "squid",
"cake", pear" ]
```

Pop and Shift

While push and unshift both let you add data to the end and beginning of your array, respectively, pop and shift let you do the same but for removal. To illustrate this, let's look at an example. If we want to remove the value "pear" which we added to the end of our array, we simply need to run pop() on it:

```
let myArr = [ "banana", "apple", "squid", "cake", "pear" ]
myArr.pop()
console.log(myArr) // [ "banana", "apple", "squid", "cake" ]
```

Similarly, if we want to remove "banana" from the beginning of the array, we can use `shift()`:

```
let myArr = [ "banana", "apple", "squid", "cake" ]
myArr.shift()
console.log(myArr) // [ "apple", "squid", "cake" ]
```

Splice

Adding and removing elements from the start and end of an array is useful, but more often than not, we'll want to change something in the middle of an array. To do this, we can use another method called `splice()`. Unlike the methods we have seen so far, `splice()` takes a couple of arguments, although only one is required. Since only one argument is required, the syntax for splice can look like any of the following variations:

```
someArray.splice(start)
someArray.splice(start, end)
someArray.splice(start, end, item1)
someArray.splice(start, end, item1, item2, item3 ... itemN)
```

The arguments we give to splice provide information to the function on what we want to do. These arguments are defined in the following:

- `start` (required) – This is the position in the array you want to start the splice at. If it's a negative number, it will count back from the end of the array.

- `end` (optional) – This is how many items you want to delete. If you only want to insert something, then set this to 0. If you don't put a number here, then all elements after the start position will be deleted.

- `item1 ... itemN` (optional) – These are array items that will be inserted after the start position. You can add as many as you like here, all comma-separated.

If we only use the first argument in splice, then every element after a certain point in the array will be deleted, as is shown in the following example:

```
let myArr = [ "banana", "apple", "squid", "cake" ]
myArr.splice(1)
console.log(myArr) // [ "banana", "apple" ]
```

If we define an end value, we can delete items in the middle of an array instead. For example, let's delete "apple" and "octopus":

```
let myArr = [ "banana", "apple", "squid", "cake" ]
myArr.splice(0, 2)
console.log(myArr) // [ "banana", "cake" ]
```

Finally, if we use the arguments after start and end, we can add new items in specific parts of our array. Let's add "strawberry" and "box" in between "banana" and "cake", using the third and fourth arguments. Any argument given after the end argument will be added to the array at the start position:

```
let myArr = [ "banana", "apple", "squid", "cake" ]
myArr.splice(0, 2)
console.log(myArr) // [ "banana", "cake" ]
myArr.splice(1, 0, "strawberry", "box")
console.log(myArr) // [ "banana", "strawberry", "box", "cake" ]
```

Objects

Now that we've covered arrays, let's move onto objects. Objects are similar to arrays, but they differ in that they have defined keys. Objects are arguably the most important thing you can understand in JavaScript, and they lead into more advanced concepts on how we write and structure our code. In this section, we'll look into how objects work and how they are used more broadly in prototypical inheritance, which is the main programming style in

JavaScript. JavaScript objects look a lot like what are called "Dictionaries" in other languages and consist of defined key–value pairs. They can be defined within curly brackets {}, as is shown in the following example:

```
let myObject = {
    "key": "value",
    "someKey": 5,
    "anotherKey" : true
}
```

This object has three keys and three values assigned to each of those keys. Keys have to be unique, but values do not, and objects can be as big as you'd like them to be.

The curly brackets {}, are known as the "object literal" notation – so as you'd expect, it is the equivalent of writing "new Object" (just like for Arrays). Since objects have keys, however, if we want to use the constructor to define an object, we need to write all the keys and values out separately and attach them to the object, making the object literal notation infinitely easier to use. In the following example, we create the same object as we did in our previous example, but we use the object constructor instead of the object literal:

```
// Objects defined without the object literal notation
// are harder to define, since we need to define each
// key separately.
let myObject = new Object()
myObject.key = "value"
myObject.someKey = 5
myObject.anotherKey = true
```

You can think of objects as miniature databases of information, where each unique key references some piece of data. Objects have these common characteristics:

1. The keys must be either a string, number, or symbols (a special unique identifier in JavaScript).

2. The values can be of any type and contain any data (objects, arrays, numbers, strings, functions, etc.)

3. Objects are resizable and can be mutated (unlike other data in JavaScript).

Remember: Arrays are objects too! So all of these properties apply to them as well.

Accessing Object Data

Just as we saw with arrays, we can use square brackets to access data on an object. You can see an illustration of how that works in the following example. The outcome of this code can also be seen in Figure 3-1.

```
let myObject = {
    "key": "value",
    "someKey": 5,
    "anotherKey" : true
}
console.log(myObject["key"]) // shows 'value'
```

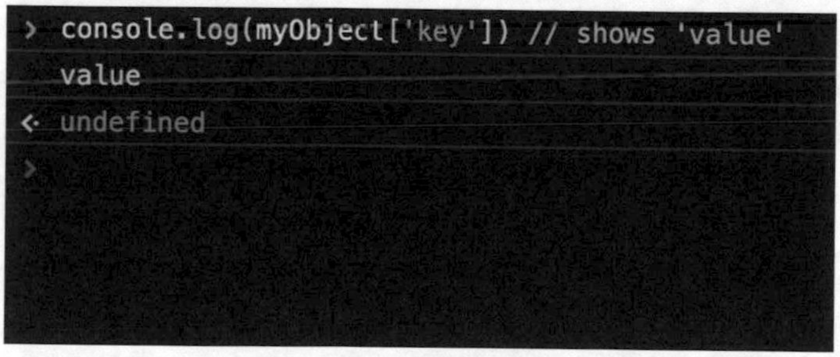

Figure 3-1. *Using the square bracket notation, we can access the value of any key on an object in JavaScript*

The Dot Notation vs. Square Brackets with Objects

Another way to access object values is by using the dot . instead. This is shown in the following example:

```
let myObject = {
    "key": "value",
    "someKey": 5,
    "anotherKey" : true
}
console.log(myObject.key) // shows 'value'
```

When we use square brackets, we must use quotation marks if the key is a string ("key", not key), but the same is not true for the dot notation.

As an example of this, consider the following code. With square brackets, the keyName variable is used if we omit the quotation marks. However, when using the dot, JavaScript will look for a key on myObject called keyName, which of course, returns undefined. Therefore, both square brackets and dot notation have different utilities when accessing objects:

```
let myObject = {
    "key": "value",
    "someKey": 5,
    "anotherKey" : true
}
let keyName = "key"
console.log(myObject[keyName]) // shows "value"
console.log(myObject.keyName) // shows undefined
```

You can see this code running in Figure 3-2.

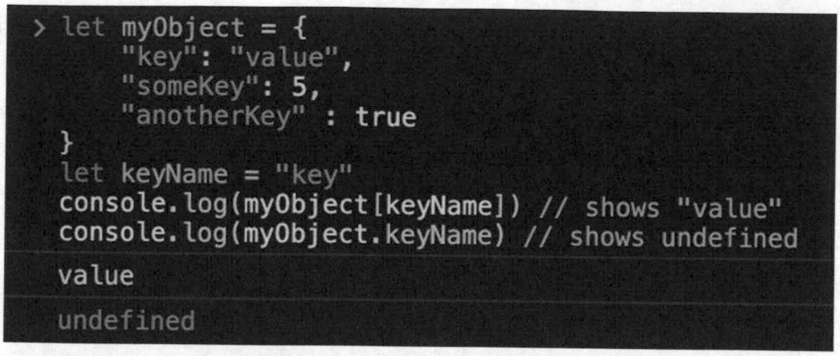

```
> let myObject = {
    "key": "value",
    "someKey": 5,
    "anotherKey" : true
}
let keyName = "key"
console.log(myObject[keyName]) // shows "value"
console.log(myObject.keyName) // shows undefined

value

undefined
```

Figure 3-2. *Using the square bracket notation, we can access the value of any key on an object in JavaScript*

Accessing objects   While we are exploring object access here, we've already used objects in Chapters 1 and 2. When we used `console.log`, `console` is the object, and `log` is a property on the console object. If you try to `console.log console` itself, you'll be able to see the entire object in your console!

Destructuring Objects

We've now covered the many ways you can access data on an object. Another useful way to do this is by destructuring the object. Destructuring objects works by allowing us to split the object into a set of variables, each of which can be used independently. To illustrate this, let's look at an example. First, let's create a simple object:

```
const myObj = {
    z: 5,
    y: 4,
    x: 3
}
```

We can now access parts of this object by destructuring them in into variables, as shown in the following example:

```
const myObj = {
    z: 5,
    y: 4,
    x: 3
}
const { x, y } = myObj
console.log(y) // 4
```

This is a useful way to take an object and only access the bits you need via variables. It's particularly common when unwrapping external packages in Node.js, but it's also widely used in front-end client JavaScript too. Destructuring can even give default values to undefined ones. If a value is found to be undefined when destructuring, the default will be used instead:

```
const myObj = {
    z: undefined,
    y: 4,
    x: 3
}
const { z = 5 } = myObj
console.log(z) // 5
```

The variable names you use when destructuring must match the property names, unless you are destructuring an array. In that case, you can call your variables anything you like:

```
const [a, b ] = [1, 2]
console.log(a) // 1
```

You can unwrap a set of objects together using the three dots operator, as shown in the following example:

```
const myObj = {
    z: undefined,
    y: 4,
    x: 3
}
const { x, ...rest } = myObj
// Only shows z and y: { z: undefined, y: 4 }
console.log(rest)
```

Object Mutability

As we've discussed previously, objects are mutable even if contained within a const variable. We can update any key on an object to something else by using an equals sign to set it to something completely different:

```
let myObject = {
    "key": "value",
    "someKey": 5,
    "anotherKey" : true
}

// Let's update one of the keys on myObject
myObject["key"] = "NEW VALUE"
console.log(myObject["key"]) // shows 'NEW VALUE'
```

Adding new keys can also be achieved by directly defining them in code, as shown in the following example:

```
let myObject = {
    "key": "value",
    "someKey": 5,
    "anotherKey" : true
}
```

```
// Let's update one of the keys on myObject
myObject["aNewKey"] = "Some Value"
console.log(myObject["aNewKey"]) // shows 'Some Value'
```

Objects may also contain other objects within them, and these can be accessed via multiple square brackets or using the dot notation if you prefer:

```
let myObject = {
    "key": {
        "key" : 5,
        "newKey" : "value"
    },
    "someKey": 5,
    "anotherKey" : true
}
```

```
console.log(myObject['key']['newKey']) // shows 'value'
console.log(myObject.key.newKey) // shows 'value'
```

Non-mutable objects

The only time an object's mutability changes is if you change it yourself. All objects have three hidden properties that configure their mutability along with their value:

- Writable – True if the property's value can be changed, false if it is read-only.

- Enumerable – True if the property will be shown in loops, false if it won't be.

- Configurable – True if the property's value can be deleted or modified, false if it cannot.

By default, all of these properties are true. Some useful utility methods exist to change these properties. For example, you can change an object to read-only by using Object.freeze, after which no property changes will affect the object. In practice, all this does is sets the object to { `writable:` `false, configurable: false` }. Another similar property, `Object.seal`, will instead set an object to { `configurable: false` }. This means existing properties can be changed but not delete, and new ones cannot be added.

In Figure 3-3, you can see how `Object.freeze` prevents an object from being modified. No errors are thrown, but the change is ignored.

```
> let myObject = { "name" : "John" }
  Object.freeze(myObject)
  myObject["age"] = 5
  myObject["name"] = "Johnny"
  console.log(myObject)
  ▶ {name: 'John'}
```

Figure 3-3. *In this image,* `Object.freeze` *means myObject can no longer be changed. If we had used Object.seal instead, then changing via myObject["name"] would have worked, while trying to add the age property would still have failed*

While in the previous examples we've applied `Object.freeze` and `Object.seal` to entire objects, individual properties each have their own enumerable, configurable, and writable properties. You can configure these settings if you define a new property using the defineProperty method instead. An example of this is shown in Figure 3-4.

```
> const myObject = {}

  Object.defineProperty(myObject, "name", {
    value: "John",
    writable: false,
  })
< ▶ {name: 'John'}
```

Figure 3-4. *In the preceding example, we create a new property called name, which is not writable. This means that the property cannot be updated. If the property was an object itself, you could still extend it, as configurable would default to true*

Spread Syntax or the "Three Dots"

We've covered a variety of methods that can be used to manipulate arrays and objects. Another useful way to manipulate objects and arrays in a specific way is through an operator known as the spread syntax or three dots, which is used widely to change arrays and objects. The spread syntax can do four things:

1. Merging arrays

2. Merging objects

3. Coercing arrays into objects

4. Passing arrays as arguments to functions

Using the spread syntax, you can quite easily merge two arrays, as shown in the following example:

```
let animals1 = [ "cats", "dogs"]
let animals2 = [ "pigeons" ]
let allAnimals = [ ...animals1, ...animals2 ]
console.log(allAnimals) // [ "cats", "dogs", "pigeons" ]
```

Objects can also be merged in the same way – but if duplicate keys are found, the second object will overwrite the first:

```
let user1 = { "name" : "John", age: 24 }
let user2 = { "name" : "Joe" }
let combineUsers = { ...user1, ...user2 }
console.log(combineUsers) // { "name" : "Joe", age: 24 }
```

Using the spread syntax on an array inside of an object literal will turn it into an object, too – where the keys are the indices of the array. This provides a simple way to convert an array to an object:

```
let animals = [ "cats", "dogs"]
let objectAnimals = { ...animals }
console.log(objectAnimals) // {0: 'cats', 1: 'dogs'}
```

Prototype-Based Programming

When we started this chapter, we mentioned that all arrays have the method `.at()`. The reason for this is that arrays are created by initiating a new instance of an array via `new Array()`. When a new instance of an array is made, it inherits all properties and methods of the `Array` object, which includes `.at()`.

Inheritance in JavaScript happens via something we call **prototypes**, a special part of all objects that allows for inheritance. While other languages use classes and object-oriented programming, the most common paradigm in JavaScript is the use of prototypes. This type of programming is called **prototype-based programming**.

All objects in JavaScript have a prototype, including arrays. You can see that if you try to console log any object. In Figure 3-5, a console log of an object I just created shows the `[[Prototype]]` property.

```
> let myObject = { "name" : "John" }
  console.log(myObject)

▼ {name: 'John'} ⓘ
    name: "John"
  ▶ [[Prototype]]: Object
```

Figure 3-5. *All objects in JavaScript have a prototype property*

I already mentioned that all arrays "inherit" standard methods, like `.at()`:

```
let myArray = [ "one", 2, "three", "four" ]
let arrayLength = myArray.length

console.log(myArray.at(-1)) // shows 'four'
```

But **how** do all arrays "inherit" the `.at()` method? Well first, it's important to remember that we said square brackets act as "syntactic sugar" for the array constructor:

```
let myArray = new Array("one", 2, "three", "four")
```

Here, we are telling JavaScript we want to make a new instance of the `Array` object. Since array is just a predefined object in JavaScript, it already has its own prototype.

When we tell JavaScript to make a new instance of `Array`, it takes whatever JavaScript defines an "`Array`" object as and makes a brand-new copy of it, including any methods, prototypes and properties.

On this prototype is where we find properties like `.length`, and methods like `.at()`. This isn't very obvious when using the square bracket array literal notation, but it's much clearer when you use `new Array`.

Before we go any deeper, let's test this out. You can use `console.log()` on `Array.prototype` to find all the methods that exist on the `Array` object – which are inherited by all arrays. At the very top, you'll see `.at()`, but there are a lot more. All of these methods are accessible on all `Arrays` since all `Arrays` are created using either `new Array` or square brackets (which is the same thing as `new Array`). An example of the response to console logging this can be seen in Figure 3-6.

```
> console.log(Array.prototype)
  ▼[constructor: f, at: f, concat: f, copyWith
    ▶ at: f at()
    ▶ concat: f concat()
    ▶ constructor: f Array()
    ▶ copyWithin: f copyWithin()
    ▶ entries: f entries()
    ▶ every: f every()
    ▶ fill: f fill()
    ▶ filter: f filter()
    ▶ find: f find()
    ▶ findIndex: f findIndex()
    ▶ findLast: f findLast()
```

Figure 3-6. *Console logging any object in JavaScript can be quite revealing – and doing so on array shows us all possible methods we can use on every array. Remember this tip if you get confused when writing JavaScript!*

Although so far we've been talking about arrays, the same is true for all objects. Since all objects are new instances of a standard "object" type, you can find all standard object methods by using console.log(Object. prototype).

Prototypical Inheritance

We are now getting relatively familiar with objects and arrays and hopefully gaining an understanding of how arrays and objects both get their methods and properties. We also know how to access object properties. For example, we know that given the following code, we could access the property key by typing myObject.key:

```
let myObject = {
    "key": "value",
    "someKey": {
        "someOtherKey" : 5
```

```
    },
    "anotherKey" : true
}
```

We also saw earlier that we could use the `Array.at()` method to get an array item at a specific index:

```
let myArray = [ "one", 2, "three", "four" ]

console.log(myArray.at(-1)) // shows 'four'
```

This may seem strange, since this method exists on `Array.prototype`, not `Array`. So given what we know about how we access objects, shouldn't the preceding code be `myArray.prototype.at(-1)`?

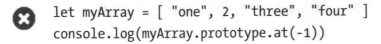

```
let myArray = [ "one", 2, "three", "four" ]
console.log(myArray.prototype.at(-1))
```

Well, the answer is of course no, and the preceding code will actually produce an error. To understand why, we have to learn about how JavaScript checks for properties on an object, as well as how JavaScript copies prototypes to new instances. When we write `myArray.at(-1)`, JavaScript does the following:

1. Checks the object, `myArray`, for the property `at`.

2. If it doesn't exist, checks the object `myArray`'s prototype for the property.

3. If it still doesn't exist, checks the object `myArray`'s prototype's prototype for the property.

4. Keeps doing this until no more `prototypes` exist, at which point it will return `undefined`.

That's why `myArray.at(-1)` works, but it doesn't exactly explain why `myArray.prototype.at(-1)` work. The reason for this is that `myArray.prototype` is undefined. If you try console logging a new array, you'll find a `[[Prototype]]` property, but no prototype property. Since arrays inherit these methods in a special prototype section and not on the object itself, we can't access methods via `myArray.prototype`. This can be seen in Figure 3-7.

```
> let myArray = [ 1, 2, 3, 4 ]
  console.log(myArray)
  ▼ (4) [1, 2, 3, 4] ℹ
      0: 1
      1: 2
      2: 3
      3: 4
      length: 4
    ▶ [[Prototype]]: Array(0)
```

Figure 3-7. *While a new array will inherit all prototype properties and methods from its parent, they do not exist within a* `prototype` *property. Instead, they sit in a special area called* `[[Prototype]]`

[[Prototype]] vs. prototype (and __proto__)

The reason why `myArray.prototype` is undefined is because prototype methods and properties which are inherited exist on a special, hidden property called `[[Prototype]]`.

When we create a new instance of array, it points this new array's `[[Prototype]]` to the `Array` constructor's `Array.prototype`.

While that is clear, there also exists another property called `__proto__` to further confuse matters. You will find this when trying to console logging `Object.prototype`. You may have thought, "*That is oddly similar to prototype,*" and you wouldn't be wrong that the two are related. The `__proto__` property is actually just a way to access the underlying `[[Prototype]]` of an object. It is a **deprecated** feature, meaning you shouldn't use it. If you do use it, it's very slow, and since it's not a standard part of the JavaScript specification, you might run into some unexpected problems. A console log for `Object.prototype` where you can see the `__proto__` property can be found in Figure 3-8.

```
> console.log(Object.prototype)
  ▼{constructor: ƒ, __defineGetter__: ƒ, __defineSetter__: ƒ, hasOwnP
   ▶ constructor: ƒ Object()
   ▶ hasOwnProperty: ƒ hasOwnProperty()
   ▶ isPrototypeOf: ƒ isPrototypeOf()
   ▶ propertyIsEnumerable: ƒ propertyIsEnumerable()
   ▶ toLocaleString: ƒ toLocaleString()
   ▶ toString: ƒ toString()
   ▶ valueOf: ƒ valueOf()
   ▶ __defineGetter__: ƒ __defineGetter__()
   ▶ __defineSetter__: ƒ __defineSetter__()
   ▶ __lookupGetter__: ƒ __lookupGetter__()
   ▶ __lookupSetter__: ƒ __lookupSetter__()
     __proto__: (...)
   ▶ get __proto__: ƒ __proto__()
   ▶ set __proto__: ƒ __proto__()
  <· undefined
  >
```

Figure 3-8. *The prototype of an object has a property called* `__proto__`*, as shown earlier*

In summary:

- The `prototype` property found on `array` and `object` is a set of all properties inherited onto arrays and objects `[[Prototype]]`s when we make new instances of them (with array or object literal notation, or `new Array/Object()`).

- The [[Prototype]] is a hidden property, which exists on all objects and can be seen by using console.log(). When you make a new instance of an Array or Object, the [[Prototype]] of that new instance points toward the prototype property of Array/Object.

- The __proto__ property is a deprecated way of accessing an objects [[Prototype]]. It is strongly discouraged and is not implemented the same in every browser or JavaScript engine.

Object Shallow and Deep Copies

When data is created inside a variable, the variable points toward that data, rather than containing it. When we've used array methods earlier in this chapter, we seemed to modify the original array. For example, using splice on an array changes its value when we try to console log it:

```
let myArr = [ "banana", "apple", "squid", "cake" ]
myArr.splice(0, 2)
console.log(myArr) // [ "banana", "cake" ]
```

This seems to make a lot of sense. The variable myVar has changed, so of course, the original data should be different. However, things begin to get tricky when you put the splice into another variable. When we do that, you'll find that the two variables have different values on the console log:

```
let myArr = [ "lightning", "search", "key", "bolt" ]
let newArr = myArr.slice(2, 3);
console.log(myArr); // [ "lightning", "search", "key", "bolt" ]
console.log(newArr); // [ "key" ]
```

Shouldn't an update to myArr using splice cause the original value to change too so that both myArr and newArr are the same? In practice, it doesn't work that way, and the reason why is actually another JavaScript quirk.

JavaScript makes what is known as a "shallow copy" of data when you use any array method. That means you have two "references," which point to the same underlying data. To visualize this, see Figure 3-9.

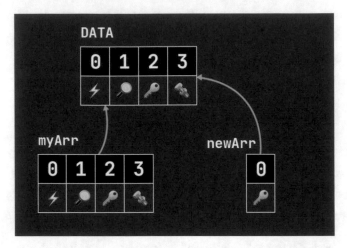

Figure 3-9. *In the preceding image, the underlying "DATA" is the "value." Then myArr and newArr are both references to that data*

While the values stored in myArr and newArr are now different, they still reference the same underlying data. The data in the reference is different since it has been changed by the slice method. Since we stored the slice output on a variable, the underlying data never changed. This can make it seem like both variables are working independently, but they are not!

If you try experimenting with this, you might get even more confused because JavaScript only updates the underlying "value" (i.e., the DATA in Figure 3-4) in certain circumstances. For example, updating the value of only newArr, seems to only affect newArr:

```
let myArr = [ "lightning", "search", "key", "bolt" ]
let newArr = myArr.slice(2, 3)
```

```
newArr[2] = "lightning"
console.log(myArr) // [ "lightning", "search", "key", "bolt" ]
console.log(newArr) // [ "key", empty, "lightning" ]
```

So if they are both working from the same data under the hood, why does this not update the underlying value of our data? That's because of something that also seems strange, which is that if you use square brackets specifically, it only assigns data to the shallow copy! If you instead use the dot notation, like in situations where an object is in your array, both the shallow and original will change since changing a property changes the underlying value:

```
let myArr = [ { items: [ "search" ]}, "search", "key", "bolt" ]
let newArr = myArr.slice(0, 3)

// Update arrayOneSlice
newArr[0].items = [ "lightning" ]

console.log(myArr) // [ {items: [ "lightning" ]}, "search",
"key", "bolt" ]
console.log(newArr); // [ {items: [ "lightning" ]},
"search", "key" ]
```

You can see in the previous example that changing newArr[0].items affects both the shallow copy and the original. It's important that you are careful when using methods like slice since you could end up changing your data in ways you never expected.

The solution to avoid this problem entirely is to create a "deep copy" of the original. That means an entirely new reference in memory is made so that both variables can work independently. This is quite computationally expensive when working with large objects, so only use it when you need to. The recommended way to do this is to use the structuredClone function:

```
let myArray = [ 1, 2, 3, 4 ];
let deepCopy = structuredClone(myArray);
```

Deep copies give you certainty. In the previous example, if you apply any methods to deepCopy, it will only affect deepCopy. The function, structuredClone, can be used on any object or array to ensure it is a deep copy rather than a shallow one.

Summary

In this chapter, we've covered the fundamentals of objects and arrays. We've shown you how to construct your own objects and arrays, and then how to mutate them using a variety of methods and operators. In addition to this, we've looked at how prototypical inheritance works and how objects form the backbone of JavaScript's main programming paradigm, prototype-based programming. We've also looked at the variety of ways you can manipulate or access objects and how you can limit access to objects via hidden properties like configurable. Finally, we look at some of the quirks related to working with objects, such as deep and shallow copies.

In future chapters, we'll build on the themes we have learned here by introducing new concepts.

CHAPTER 4

Loops and Iterables

As we start writing more complicated code, it is both necessary and desired to not repeat ourselves. This concept in programming is known as DRY, or **D**on't **R**epeat **Y**ourself. This concept becomes really important when we're working with large datasets. For example, imagine you find yourself wanting to create 10 new rows on a table. You *could* write the same code ten times in a row, but that would neither be efficient nor a good use of your time.

To avoid repeating ourselves, we use loops and iteration, and JavaScript has a number of ways to perform both of these tasks. In this chapter, we'll be looking at how we can add these on top of what we've learned so far.

Loops

There are three forms of loops in JavaScript. The first we will look at is the `while` clause. The `while` clause accepts one logical statement, and *while* that logical statement is true, the code inside curly brackets will continue to be executed. In the following example, the result is that `console.log` will run ten times:

```
let x = 1
while(x < 10) {
    console.log(x)
    ++x
}
```

© Jonathon Simpson 2023
J. Simpson, *How JavaScript Works*, https://doi.org/10.1007/978-1-4842-9738-4_4

Since we don't want a while loop to run indefinitely, we often adjust the variable or condition each time the while look runs. In the previous example, every time while runs, we also use the ++ operator to add 1 to x. ++x is shorthand, and it's the equivalent to writing x += 1. The opposite of ++ is -- which subtracts 1 from a variable. If you didn't do this, you'd create an infinite loop, which would ultimately cause your code to break! A summary of how the while loop above works is shown in Figure 4-1.

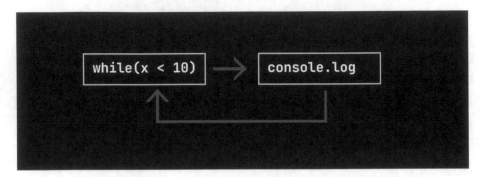

Figure 4-1. *A while loop will keep executing code until the logical statement is no longer true. In this example, if you do not add or multiply something by x, the logical statement will always remain true, leading to an infinite loop and an error*

The result of our preceding loop is shown in Figure 4-2. Since (x < 10) remains true until x has had 10 added to it, we get 10 new lines on the console log.

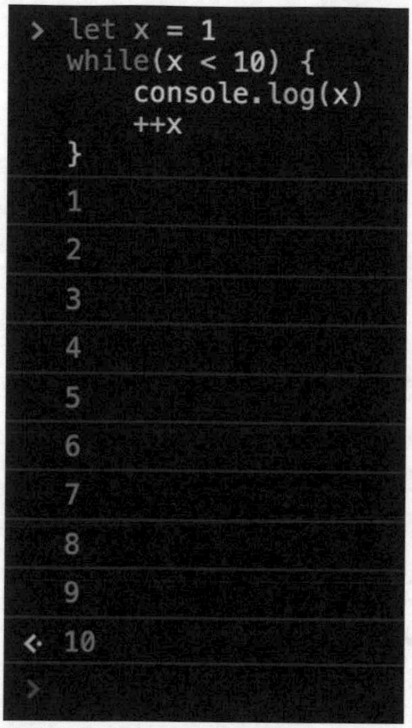

```
>  let x = 1
   while(x < 10) {
       console.log(x)
       ++x
   }
   1
   2
   3
   4
   5
   6
   7
   8
   9
<· 10
>
```

Figure 4-2. *By using the* while *loop, we can do an action multiple times, without having to write out what we want to do many times over. It's important to modify a participant in your* while *condition; otherwise, you may get an infinite loop*

An alternative way of performing a while loop using similar syntax is with do...while. It works the same way, except the condition is checked after the code is run, meaning the code will **always** run at least once. In the following example, the code runs one console log saying "hello world." With a normal while loop, it would not run at all since x is not less than 1:

```
let x = 1
do {
    console.log("hello world")
} while(x < 1)
```

The final way we can perform a loop is with a for statement. A for statement combines the variable definition, logical statement, and modification all in one statement. In the following example, we recreate the while statement from Figure 4-1, but using for instead:

```
for(let x = 1; x < 10; ++x) {
    console.log(x)
}
```

The for loop is tidier than a while loop since all of its conditions are confined to one line. Functionally, though, it does the same thing that while does. The modification defined in the for loop, that being ++x, will only run after the body of the loop has been run. Table 4-1 summarizes how the for loop works.

Table 4-1. *A breakdown of the for statement*

Code	Section	Description
for	Initiator	Initiates the for loop.
let x = 1	Variable	Defines a single variable to be used in the for loop.
x < 10	Condition	While this continues to be true, the body of the for loop will run.
++x	Modifier	Some modification that occurs. Does not need to include the variable, but usually does. Could also be something like x += 2.
console. log(x)	Body	Runs while the condition remains true.

Break and Continue in Loops

Sometimes if a certain condition is met in a loop, we will want the loop to stop running again immediately. For example, suppose we are adding 2 to a value and want the loop to break if it hits the value 10. In that case, we can use an if statement to conditionally break the loop:

```
for(let x = 0; x < 20; x += 2) {
    if(x === 10) break
    console.log(x)
}
```

Since we break before the console log, this loop only shows 0, 2, 4, 6, 8. Another similar concept is continue, which instead of breaking the entire loop, only breaks the current iteration.

```
for(let x = 0; x < 20; x += 2) {
    if(x === 10) continue
    console.log(x)
}
```

Using continue only breaks the current iteration, so the preceding code will now show 0, 2, 4, 6, 8, 12, 14, 16, 18 – only skipping a console log on the loop when the value is 10.

Loop Labels

As our code gets more complicated, we can end up with loops inside of loops. That can lead to some interesting problems when using breaks, since break and continue do not know which loop you want to break or continue on.

To solve this, we can use labels to define which loop is supposed to break and continue. Here's an example of a labeled loop, where I use the labels xLoop and yLoop to refer to the outer and inner loop, respectively:

```
xLoop: for(let x = 1; x < 4; x += 2) {
    yLoop: for(let y = 1; y < 4; y += 2) {
        console.log(`xLoop: ${x * y}`)
    }
    console.log(`yLoop: ${x}`)
}
```

If we wanted to break xLoop from within yLoop, we can write break xLoop. This has the effect of breaking all of xLoop if the value of x * y is 4, preventing any console.log(x) lines. You can see the output of this in Figure 4-3:

```
xLoop: for(let x = 1; x < 4; x += 2) {
    yLoop: for(let y = 1; y < 4; y += 2) {
        if(x === 1 || x === 3) break xLoop;
        console.log(`xLoop: ${x * y}`)
    }
    console.log(`yLoop: ${x}`)
}
```

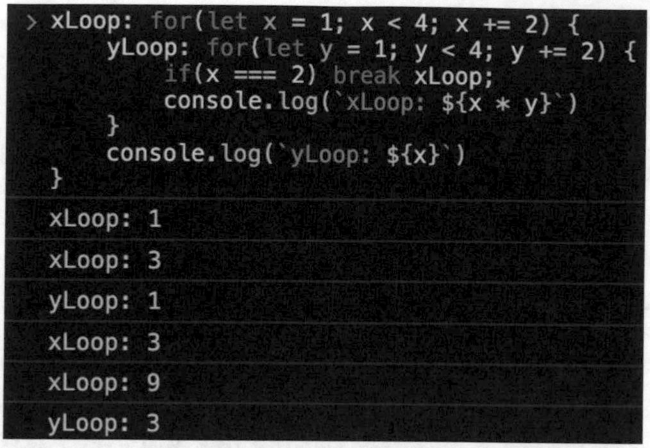

```
> xLoop: for(let x = 1; x < 4; x += 2) {
      yLoop: for(let y = 1; y < 4; y += 2) {
          if(x === 2) break xLoop;
          console.log(`xLoop: ${x * y}`)
      }
      console.log(`yLoop: ${x}`)
}
xLoop: 1
xLoop: 3
yLoop: 1
xLoop: 3
xLoop: 9
yLoop: 3
```

Figure 4-3. *In this example, when x is equal to 2, xLoop is broken. That means the whole loop is only run twice. If you broke yLoop instead when x was 2, then xLoop would continue to run, while yLoop would have been stopped*

Note   While I am using the labels xLoop and yLoop in the previous example, you can label your loops in any way you see fit – these are just made-up names!

Iteration

When using loops, we are typically using variables and logical statements to iterate through statements until they stop returning true. This stops us from repeating ourselves and simplifies our code.

In the previous chapter, we spoke about how objects and arrays act as a store of data in JavaScript. Eventually, we'll want to use the data contained by them in our code. We can access each individually, but what if we want to do something with all items in an array or object? We could write them out on separate lines, as is shown in the following example, but this quickly becomes unmanageable as the arrays and objects become bigger:

```
let myArray = [ "banana", "pineapples", "strawberries" ]
console.log(`I have 1 ${myArray[0]}`)
console.log(`I have 2 ${myArray[1]}`)
console.log(`I have 3 ${myArray[2]}`)
```

To solve this problem, some data types in JavaScript are iterable. For example, arrays and strings are both iterable, but objects are not. Other types of data like maps and sets are also iterable, but we'll cover those in much more depth in future chapters.

Iterables and For Loops

Iterable data can have their values fully extracted with the for...of or for...in loop, which will assign each element of an iterable to a variable.

In the following example, "item" refers to each individual item in the array. Each item will be console logged onto a separate line. You can see what this looks like in Figure 4-4.

```
let x = [ "lightning", "apple", "squid", "speaker" ]

for(let item of x) {
    console.log(item)
}
```

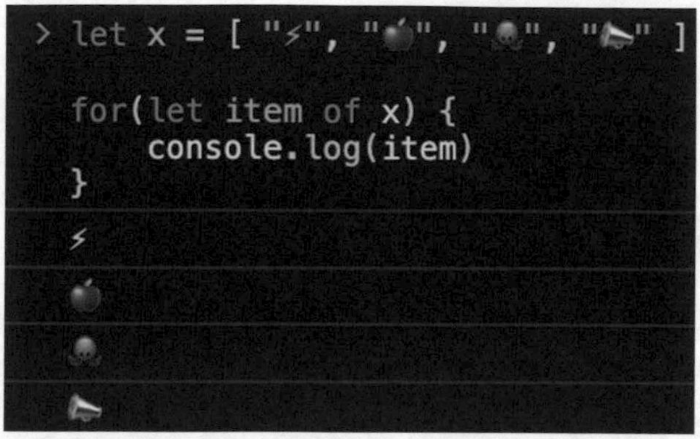

```
> let x = [ "⚡", "🍎", "💀", "📢" ]

for(let item of x) {
    console.log(item)
}

⚡

🍎

💀

📢
```

Figure 4-4. *The* `for...of` *loop will allow us to access every item of an array or iterable, as shown in the preceding image*

`for...in`, on the other hand, will refer to the index, and not the item itself. In the following example, the output is 0, 1, 2, 3, whereas in `for...of`, it was lightning, apple, squid, speaker as the output:

```
let x = [ "lightning", "apple", "squid", "speaker" ]

for(let item in x) {
    console.log(item)
}
```

`for...of` and `for...in` differ in the way they handle undefined values. For example, consider the following example where an array consists of only one array item at location 5. When using `for...of`, it will return 4 undefined values, followed by "some value":

```
let x = []
x[5] = "some value"

for(let item of x) {
    console.log(item)
    // Will show:
```

77

```
    // undefined, undefined, undefined, undefined, undefined
    // "some value"
}
```

With for...in, we only get indices and not array values, so it therefore omits any undefined values:

```
for(let item in x) {
    console.log(item)
    // Will show: 5
}
```

Array forEach methods

While not all types implement a method for iteration, arrays do. To help with iteration, arrays also have a special method called forEach. This method accepts a function with three arguments, as shown in the following example:

```
let x = [ "lightning", "apple", "squid", "speaker" ]
x.forEach(function(item, index, array) {
    console.log(`${item} is at index ${index}`)
})
```

The forEach method provides the index, item, and entire array to you at each iteration in your array. While this method is useful, it is slower than a for loop – so using a for loop when you can is your best bet.

String Iteration

Since strings are also iterable, for...of and for...in also work on them. In the following example, using for...of on the string "hello" produces an output of all characters in that string. The following code console logs individually each letter, so h,e,l,l,o. You can see this output in Figure 4-5.

```
for(let item of "hello") {
    console.log(item)
}
```

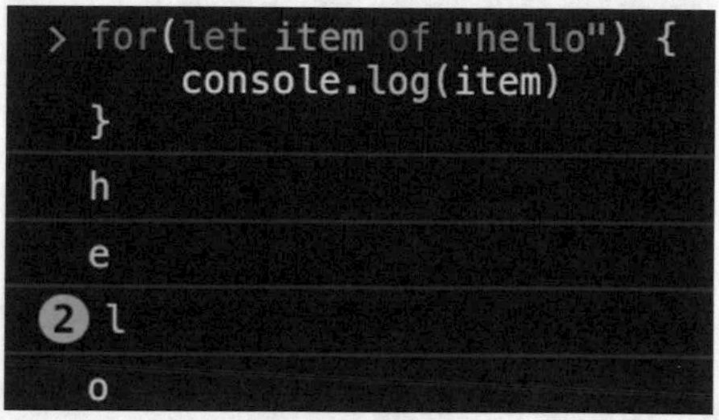

Figure 4-5. *Using* for...of *on a string will also iterate through each character in that string. If you use* for...in, *you will get a number on each line for each letter*

Iteration Protocol

In the previous chapter, we discussed how different data types, like arrays, inherit from a prototype. This is called prototypical inheritance.

When we define an array using new Array() or the square bracket notation, we are making a new instance of Array, which inherits many methods and properties from Array.prototype. Any data type, like arrays or strings, which have iterability, will inherit a property called Symbol. iterator from their prototype chain. This is known as the iteration protocol. All types which have the iteration protocol are iterable. The iteration protocol is therefore the reason why we can use for...in and for...of on arrays and strings. You can see iteration protocol property in Figure 4-6.

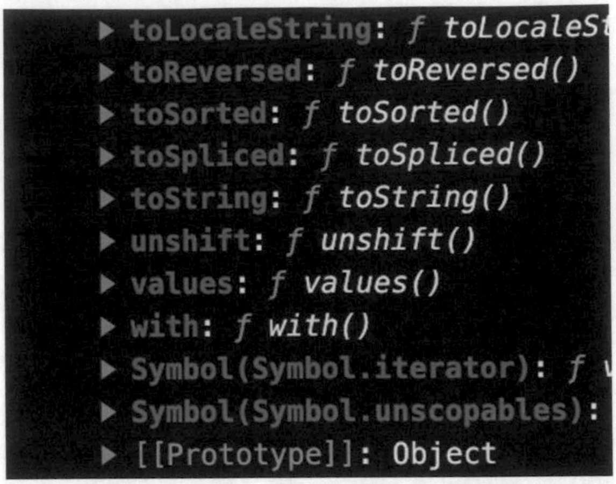

```
  ▶ toLocaleString: ƒ toLocaleSt
  ▶ toReversed: ƒ toReversed()
  ▶ toSorted: ƒ toSorted()
  ▶ toSpliced: ƒ toSpliced()
  ▶ toString: ƒ toString()
  ▶ unshift: ƒ unshift()
  ▶ values: ƒ values()
  ▶ with: ƒ with()
  ▶ Symbol(Symbol.iterator): ƒ
  ▶ Symbol(Symbol.unscopables):
  ▶ [[Prototype]]: Object
```

Figure 4-6. *You can see the iterator protocol by console logging an iterable's prototype, like* `console.log(Array.prototype)`

Another cool feature, which comes with the iteration protocol, is that they allow the iterable to be stepped through. You can do this by accessing the iteration protocol key, `Symbol.iterator`, directly. Since `Symbol.iterator` is just another key inherited from `Array.prototype`, we can access it just as we would have run `myArray.at(-1)`:

```
let myArray = [ "lightning", "apple", "squid", "speaker" ]
let getIterator = myArray[Symbol.iterator]()
console.log(getIterator)
```

`Symbol.iterator` is two words separated by a dot, so we have to access it via square brackets. We also run it as a function by sticking () at the end since it is actually a function. The results of this can be seen in Figure 4-7.

```
> let myArray = [ "⚡", "🍎", "🦑", "🔊" ]
  let getIterator = x[Symbol.iterator]()
  console.log(getIterator)
  ▶ Array Iterator {}
```

Figure 4-7. *By accessing the* Symbol.iterator, *we create a new object called an* Array Iterator. *This iterator allows us to step through an iterable*

Inside Array Iterator's [[Prototype]], you'll find a method called next(). This function allows you to iterate by one item at a time and remembers where in the sequence you last left it. For example, running getIterator.next() will give you an object containing whether the iteration is done (which is only true if you have iterated through all values) and the value of the next item in the array:

```
let myArray = [ "lightning", "apple", "squid", "speaker" ]
let getIterator = myArray[Symbol.iterator]()
console.log(getIterator.next()) // {value: 'lightning',
                                            done: false}
```

If you keep running next(), you'll keep getting the next item, as is shown in the following example:

```
let myArray = [ "lightning", "apple", "squid", "speaker" ]
let getIterator = myArray[Symbol.iterator]()
console.log(getIterator.next()) // {value: 'lightning',
                                            done: false}
console.log(getIterator.next()) // {value: 'apple',
                                            done: false}
console.log(getIterator.next()) // {value: 'squid',
                                            done: false}
console.log(getIterator.next()) // {value: 'speaker',
                                            done: true}
```

```
console.log(getIterator.next()) // {value: undefined,
                                        done: true}
```

Objects Are Not Iterable by Default

If you try to console log Object.prototype, you'll find no Symbol.
iterator property, which implies objects are not iterable. The main
reason why objects are not iterable by default is because they contain both
*key*s and *value*s. Deciding which to iterate upon or how to format that
iteration is something that JavaScript leaves to you.

Fortunately, there is an easy way to iterate through an object, and
that is to convert it to an iterable data type, like an array. There are three
methods to do this:

- Object.keys(), which extracts all keys as an array

- Object.values(), which extracts all values as an array

- Object.entries(), which extracts all keys and arrays
  as an array of key–value pairs

We haven't seen these object methods before, but they are all available
on the global Object object. Consider the following example, where we
have an array called myObject. We can use both Object.keys() and
Object.values() directly on this object to extract an array from each:

```
let myObject = {
    firstName: "John",
    lastName: "Doe",
    age: 140
}

let myObjectKeys = Object.keys(myObject)
console.log(myObjectKeys) //[ "firstName", "lastName", "age" ]
```

```
let myObjectValues = Object.values(myObject)
console.log(myObjectValues) //[ "John", "Doe", 140 ]
```

Once we have extracted an array, we can run this through a for loop since arrays are iterable. This is shown in the following example and also in Figure 4-8.

```
let myObject = {
    firstName: "John",
    lastName: "Doe",
    age: 140
}

let myObjectKeys = Object.keys(myObject)
for(let item of myObjectKeys) {
    console.log(item)
}
```

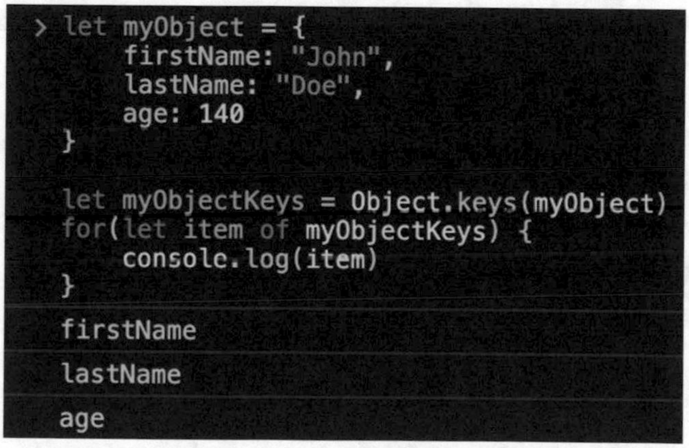

Figure 4-8. Methods like Object.keys() turn objects into iterable arrays, which we can then iterate through

Object.entries() is slightly different from Object.keys/values(), in that it creates an array of key–value pairs. You can see the output of Object. entries when applied to myObjectKeys in Figure 4-9.

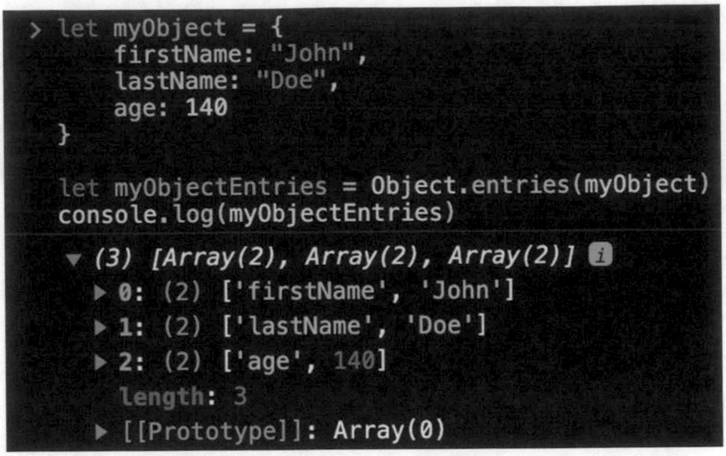

```
> let myObject = {
      firstName: "John",
      lastName: "Doe",
      age: 140
  }

  let myObjectEntries = Object.entries(myObject)
  console.log(myObjectEntries)
▼ (3) [Array(2), Array(2), Array(2)] ⓘ
  ▶ 0: (2) ['firstName', 'John']
  ▶ 1: (2) ['lastName', 'Doe']
  ▶ 2: (2) ['age', 140]
    length: 3
  ▶ [[Prototype]]: Array(0)
```

Figure 4-9. Object.entries creates an array of key–value pairs. Each key–value pair itself is an array too

Using destructuring, which we covered in a previous chapter, we can access both key and value from an object using Object.entries. In the following example, we do just that by using a for...of loop. The output of this for loop can also be seen in Figure 4-10.

```
let myObject = {
    firstName: "John",
    lastName: "Doe",
    age: 140
}

let myObjectEntries = Object.entries(myObject)
for(const [key, value] of myObjectEntries) {
    console.log(`The key ${key} has a value ${value}`)
}
```

```
> let myObject = {
     firstName: "John",
     lastName: "Doe",
     age: 140
  }

  let myObjectEntries = Object.entries(myObject)
  for(let [key, value] of myObjectEntries) {
     console.log(`The key ${key} has a value ${value}`)
  }
  The key firstName has a value John
  The key lastName has a value Doe
  The key age has a value 140
```

Figure 4-10. Key-value pairs generated by `Object.entries` can easily be accessed by using variable destructuring inside of a for loop. Here we retrieve all of the keys and values in `myObject`

Summary

In this chapter, we've covered all of the different kinds of loops in JavaScript. We've also discussed how breaks, continues, and labels work in the context of `for` loops. Looping is not just confined to logical statements, so we've also gone into a lot of detail about how to iterate over arrays, strings, and any other data type implementing the iteration protocol.

Objects, the most important data type in JavaScript, are not directly iterable. However, we can convert them into iterable arrays through methods like `Object.entries()`.

Throughout the book, we'll need to access arrays, objects, and other iterables. Understanding these concepts makes writing code more efficient, and we'll use the code we've learned here in future chapters.

CHAPTER 5

References, Values, and Memory Management

We have already alluded to the fact that variables point to certain references in memory, and we've also briefly covered how deep and shallow copies of objects exist. In this chapter, we'll be going into more depth about how memory allocation actually work. All of the concepts we will discuss in this chapter fall under a broad topic known as "**memory management**." Memory management, in simple terms, is how JavaScript allocates data we create to memory.

Introduction

To understand memory management, we need to understand "heaps" and "stacks." These are both memory concepts and are both stored in the "random access memory" or **RAM**.

Computers have a fixed amount of RAM. Since JavaScript stores data in RAM, the amount of data your JavaScript uses impacts the amount of RAM used on your computer or server. As such, it can be possible to run out of RAM if you build a sufficiently complicated JavaScript application.

© Jonathon Simpson 2023
J. Simpson, *How JavaScript Works*, https://doi.org/10.1007/978-1-4842-9738-4_5

So if the heap and stack are both stored in RAM, and they're both used for storing JavaScript data, what's the difference?

- **The stack** is a scratch space for the current JavaScript thread. JavaScript is typically single-threaded, so there is usually one stack per application. The stack is also limited in size, which is why numbers in JavaScript can only be so big.

- **The heap** is a dynamic memory store. Accessing data from the heap is more complicated, but the heap is not limited in size. As such, the heap will grow if needed.

The heap is used by JavaScript to store objects and functions. For simple variables composed of numbers, strings, and other primitive types, the stack is typically used instead. The stack also stores information on functions which will be called.

Note   JavaScript has built-in functionality known as "garbage collection" to avoid your application running out of RAM. This algorithm uses a number of different checks, like if a variable or object is no longer referenced in your code, to clear it from the memory. This goes some way to prevent you from running out of memory.

Stacks

The stack is a scratch space for the current JavaScript thread. Every time you point to a primitive type (primitive, here, meaning anything which is not an object) in JavaScript, it is added to the top of the stack. In the following code, we define variables. Non-object type data is immediately added to the top of the stack. A representation of this can be seen in Figure 5-1.

```
const SOME_CONSTANT = 5
let myNumber = 10
let myVariable = "Some Text"
```

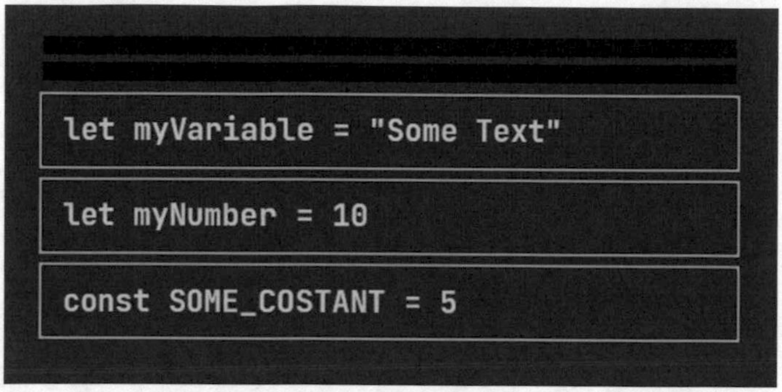

Figure 5-1. *Each new line of code is added to the stack. This includes functions*

Sometimes, when running complex code or loops, you can see the stack in action. If you exceed the stack limit, you'll get the error, `RangeError: Maximum call stack size exceeded`. Different browsers and implementations of JavaScript like Node.js have different stack sizes, but you have to be running a lot of code simultaneously to ever get this error. You may also run into this error if you accidentally run an infinite loop.

If you try to reassign a variable of primitive type, it gets added to the stack as well, even if the variables are supposedly pointing to the same value. Consider the following code, for example:

```
let myNumber = 5
let newNumber = myNumber
```

Although it seems like both of these variables should point to the same underlying value (that value being 5), JavaScript instead adds both references to the stack as individual entries with different values completely.

What that means in practice is that for any primitive or non-object value in JavaScript, a deep copy is always made. Variables will not point to the same underlying value in memory but rather appear as new copies of data, each acting independently of each other, as shown in Figure 5-2.

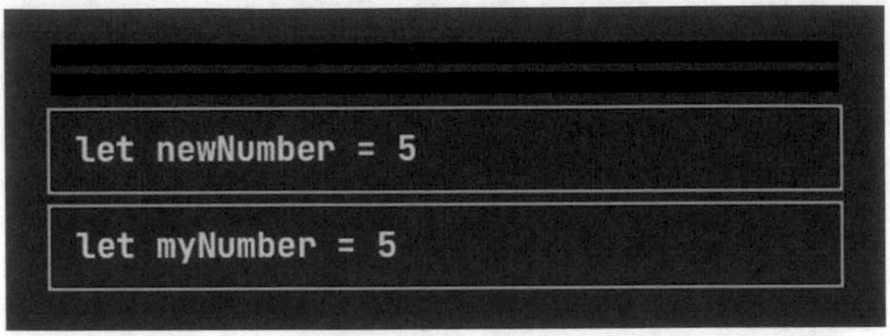

```
let newNumber = 5

let myNumber = 5
```

Figure 5-2. *Each new variable of non-object type will appear as a new reference and value on the stack*

The Event Loop

Note   In this section we will briefly go into how APIs work to show you how the event loop works. While we won't cover what APIs are and how to use them in detail here, we will go into this in future chapters. Jump ahead if you are interested in learning more about APIs.

JavaScript code only has one stack in browsers, so it is commonly described as being single-threaded. However, JavaScript can act like it has multiple threads at once on the front end via something known as Web APIs.

We use something called an API or **a**pplication **p**rogramming interfaces to let us outsource some of our computation somewhere else and wait for the response. Usually, APIs exist on a server. For example, you could hit an API for retrieving a list of articles on your website. We could then use this data in our code.

"API" sounds complicated, but it's just a URL that we can hit, which will eventually send us a response from inside our code. For example, we may hit the URL https://some-website.org/api/articles to retrieve website articles. We would then receive a response from the API with all of the articles. In a future chapter, we'll deep dive into how APIs work.

When we run an API, the server will do some computation on our behalf, but our JavaScript code will continue to run. Since the API and JavaScript code are both processing at the same time, this gives us a way to create multiple threads.

Browsers have some built-in APIs that can be called straight from your code. These are known as Web APIs, and they usually offer an interface between the code in your browser and the operating system itself. An example of a Web API is the global function, setTimeout, which lets us execute code after a certain number of seconds:

```
let myNumber = 5
setTimeout(function() {
    console.log("Hello World")
}, 1000)
```

setTimeout accepts two arguments – a callback function and a time in milliseconds, which are processed by the Web API. Most Web APIs accept a callback function, which is run on the Web API stack. This means that setTimeout is removed immediately from the main stack and only comes back to the main stack again once it has been processed.

This means that Web APIs run in parallel to the main JavaScript stack. When the callback is finished, the result is added back to the main stack, and this is mediated by something called the event loop, which decides when to add tasks to the main thread. You can see an illustration of how this works in Figure 5-3:

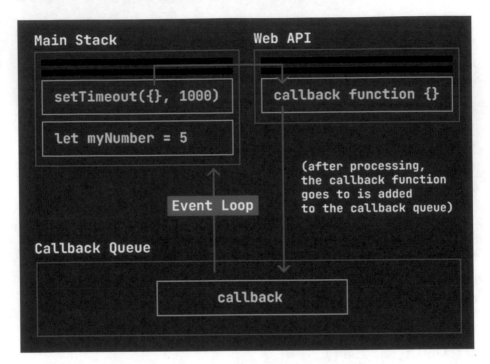

Figure 5-3. Web APIs can be used to create concurrency in JavaScript. Web APIs use callback functions, which are processed by a Web API stack, separate from other JavaScript. When processing is complete, the callback is added to the callback queue, which acts just like the stack, in that new callbacks are added to the top, and processing starts from the bottom. The event loop then mediates the callback being added to the main stack, where it can be processed like any other stack item

Note Web API functions that take a long time to run, like setTimeout, are added to the event loop as "macrotasks." Some faster Web API functions are added as "microtasks." Microtasks take priority when being added back to the main stack. Whether a Web API generates a macro or microtask is dependent on how long it takes to run!

The Heap

When we looked at objects, we covered how we can copy objects by making "deep" and "shallow" copies of them. The reason we have deep and shallow copies in JavaScript is because of how objects are stored in the heap.

While non-object types are stored in the stack only, objects are thrown into the heap, which is a more dynamic form of memory with no limit. This means that large objects will never exceed the stack limit.

Consider the following object. First, we define a new object, and then we set another variable to point to it:

```
let userOne = { name: "John Schmidt" }
let userTwo = userOne
```

While in previous examples using the stack, this type of code would lead to two new entries, this code does something slightly different. Here, the object is stored in the heap, and the stack only refers to the heap reference. The preceding code would produce something a little bit like what is shown in Figure 5-4.

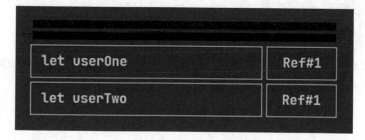

Figure 5-4. *Objects are stored in the heap, and the stack refers to the reference of that object. The reference codes used here are illustrative*

Since the variables now refer to the same object, updating one can have an effect on the other, which can cause confusion when updating arrays that you believe are deep copies, but are actually shallow copies.

Note on object types   Since functions and arrays are also of type "object," they too are stored in the heap!

Object and Reference Equality

The final complexity that JavaScript introduces by using this method of storing objects and non-objects is to do with equality. JavaScript actually has a lot of difficulty comparing the values of two different objects, and it's basically down to stacks and heaps. To understand why, consider the following code:

```
let myNumber = 5
let newNumber = 5
let newObject = { name: "John Schmidt" }
let cloneObject = { name: "John Schmidt" }
let additionalObject = newObject
```

We've just defined a bunch of variables, and in the stack, it would look a little like what's shown in Figure 5-5.

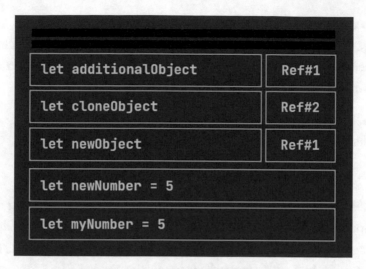

Figure 5-5. *While non-objects are made on the stack as normal, a new object creates a new reference. Even though both* cloneObject *and* newObject *have the same underlying "value," their references still differ*

So, newNumber and myNumber both have the same value and will give us a "true" value if we try to test their equality with the triple equals sign:

```
let myNumber = 5
let newNumber = 5

console.log(myNumber === newNumber) // TRUE
```

Similarly, additionalObject and newObject both refer to the same reference and will also test true for equality:

```
let newObject = { name: "John Schmidt" }
let additionalObject = newObject

console.log(newObject === additionalObject) // TRUE
```

The complexity appears when we compare `cloneObject` and `newObject`. Even though `cloneObject` has the same underlying value as `newObject`, JavaScript will compare the equality of the two references, not the underlying value itself:

```
let newObject = { name: "John Schmidt" }
let cloneObject = { name: "John Schmidt" }

console.log(newObject === cloneObject) // False
```

This is a common point of confusion for most people learning JavaScript because it's counterintuitive. When you understand heaps and stacks, it starts to make sense. `newObject` and `cloneObject` are NOT equal since they both have different references in the stack.

Comparing Object Equality

So how do you compare object equality for objects with different references in JavaScript? Well, it's not easy, and there is no built-in way to do it. Instead, you have the following options:

1. You can write your own function to compare each key and value in an object individually or find a good example online.

2. In Node.js, which we will not be covering in a lot of detail in this book, you can use the built-in `assert.deepStrictEqual(obj1, obj2)` function to compare two objects.

3. Finally, although it's not recommended, you can also convert both objects to strings using `JSON.stringify()` to compare their values. `JSON.stringify` will turn any object into a string, which

will be stored on the stack. Then, if both strings
are the same, you can assume equality. This is not
advised since this JSON method also removes some
types of data from objects, like functions. Therefore,
you cannot be sure that it will always test for
equality, making it quite unreliable.

If you're using Node.js, your best option is option 2. Otherwise, it is more advised that you write your own function (or find one online), as described in option 1.

Summary

In this chapter, we've covered a lot of basic concepts on how memory management works. We've looked at how stacks and heaps work in JavaScript. We've also touched on Web APIs and how they simulate multithreaded behavior in JavaScript. We've briefly covered APIs and Web APIs, although we will look at these in much more detail in future chapters. Topics like how JavaScript handles object equality can seem confusing and counterintuitive until we understand how objects are stored and compared differently than other data types. As such, a good understanding of memory management can help explain some of the quirks we experience when developing applications in JavaScript.

CHAPTER 6

Functions and Classes

Functions and classes are what we use to wrap certain pieces of functionality into reusable blocks. By using a function or class, we can repeat specific tasks many times without having to rewrite the code. When JavaScript was originally released, it only had functions and used prototypes for inheritance. We covered this type of inheritance when we looked at objects.

Classes came later to JavaScript, but they are largely just syntactic sugar for prototype-based inheritance. As such, many developers in JavaScript choose not to use classes and instead depend on prototypical inheritance.

As with all things in software development, it doesn't really matter if you decide to use classes, or depend on prototypical inheritance with functions. The important thing is that you are consistent throughout your projects.

Introduction to Functions

A typical function consists of three parts:

1. An input, known as arguments (although sometimes, no input is given)

2. Some code to either manipulate those inputs or perform some kind of action.

3. An output, usually related to the input. It doesn't have to be, but it's better if it is.

© Jonathon Simpson 2023
J. Simpson, *How JavaScript Works*, https://doi.org/10.1007/978-1-4842-9738-4_6

Inputs in functions are called arguments, and we return outputs using the `return` keyword. Then, when we run a function, it returns that value. If your function doesn't return anything, that is also acceptable, but better to avoid if possible.

When you don't return something from a function in JavaScript, the function will always return "undefined" by default – so the `return` keyword is technically optional in a function.

So what does a function look like? In the following example, we create a simple function that returns "Hello World" upon being run:

```
function myFunction() {
    return "Hello World"
}
console.log(myFunction())
```

We run functions by writing their names, followed by parentheses (). In the previous example, myFunction has no inputs or arguments, and all it does is return the text "Hello World." We ran this function inside console log, meaning the console would produce the text "Hello World" as shown in Figure 6-1.

Figure 6-1. *A function can be run in any context, even within another function. Since the return value of the preceding function is "Hello World," running myFunction will return that string, which can then be console logged*

Arguments are added inside the function declaration, within the round () brackets. Arguments then act as variables within the scope of the function. For example, the following function creates a sentence composed of two parts. Although not particularly useful in practice, it gives you a sense of how arguments work:

```
function words(word1, word2) {
    return word1 + " " + word2
}
console.log(words("Hello", "John")) // Hello John
console.log(words("Hello", "Jake")) // Hello Jake
console.log(words("Good bye", "Alice")) // Good bye Alice
```

As we discussed early in the book, JavaScript is dynamically typed. When we defined our preceding function, we called our arguments word1 and word2. Even though they are called this, we can provide multiple words, and JavaScript won't mind. This has its advantages, in that it's simpler, but also its disadvantages. For example, what if you were expecting only words in your function, but numbers or objects were given instead? This makes naming and control statements like if...else within functions more important in JavaScript than in other languages.

When we call a new function, it's added to the top of the stack for our program, just like a variable, as demonstrated in Figure 6-2.

Note   Functions are of type Object – so when we declare them, their data is stored in the heap. However, calling them will add them to the call stack like variables.

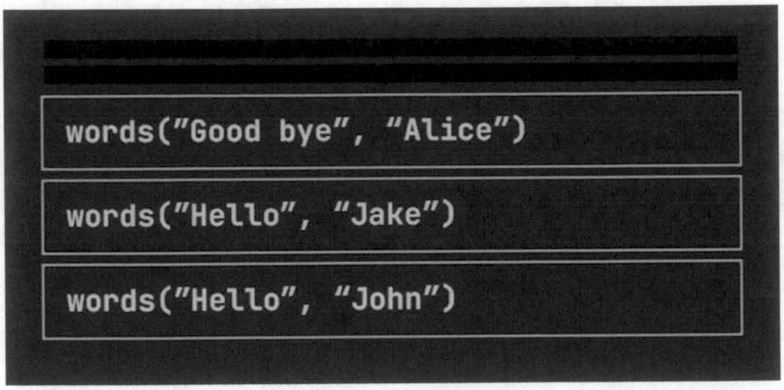

Figure 6-2. *Functions are added to the top of the stack as they are declared – just like variables*

Running Arguments with the "Three Dots"

Arguments can also be called in a function via array, using the three dots syntax, which we covered previously when we look at how to merge arrays and objects. Let's look at how that works using our previous example:

```
function words(word1, word2) {
    return word1 + " " + word2
}
let validWords = [ "Hello", "John" ]
console.log(words(...validWords)) // Hello John
```

This is really useful in the real world, where we often have data stored in arrays and objects, which we then want to pass to functions.

Alternative Ways to Call Functions

JavaScript has a tendency to have many ways to do the same thing, and functions are no exception. There are three ways to declare and call functions.

Unnamed Function Expressions

Unnamed function expressions are confusingly named since they do have a name – but the name is expressed via variable. You can define them via let or const variables – and then the variable name becomes the function name. Here is our previous example, using variables instead:

```
let words = function(word1, word2) {
    return word1 + " " + word2
}

console.log(words("Hello", "World"))
```

We can also put functions like this inside objects, allowing us to group functions together or add methods to a prototype:

```
let wordFunctions = {
    words: function(word1, word2) {
        return word1 + " " + word2
    }
}
```

In the preceding example, calling wordFunctions.words() would let us run this function.

Anonymous Functions

Anonymous functions (also sometimes referred to as Immediately Invoked Function Expression or IIFEs) are functions that actually are unnamed and are called immediately. To make it run immediately, we wrap it in round brackets and call it with double round brackets as before:

```
(function(word1, word2) {
        return word1 + " " + word2
})("Hello", "World")
```

Arguments are put in the second set of brackets so that they can be passed to the function. The use of anonymous functions is falling, but they are sometimes still used to create a separate scope to work within.

Functions with Arrow Notation

The arrow notation is another way of defining functions. This notation comes with some different functionality compared to the other function definitions we've covered. The arrow notation is called as such because it uses => to indicate where the body of the function begins.

Here is how our previous function looks with the arrow notation. When you try to call it, it works the same as our other function expressions:

```
let words = (word1, word2) => {
    return word1 + " " + word2
}
console.log(words("Hello", "John")) // Hello John
```

Arrow notation functions are different in that they don't store a unique context. To understand what that means, we first have to understand what the this keyword means in JavaScript and therefore a little bit about strict mode.

Functions and the "this" Keyword

The keyword this can be a little tricky to understand in JavaScript since it behaves differently than in other languages. The main purpose of the keyword this is to contain information on your current context.

At the top level of your code, outside of any functions, the context is "global." When we use the "this" keyword in the global context on browsers, it refers to an object called window. The window object contains lots of useful information about your current context. For example, window.innerWidth tells you the width of the user's browser window. It also contains information on mouse position, and it's where all Web APIs exist.

As such, the two console logs in the following example show the same thing:

```
:console.log(this) // Console logs window object
console.log(window) // Console logs window object
```

Given what we've said so far, when we call the this keyword inside a function, you might expect the this keyword to refer to the context of the function, but you'll find that it still shows the global this object:

```
 console.log(this) // Window { }
let words = function (word1, word2) {
    console.log(this) // Window { }
    return word1 + " " + word2
}
```

This doesn't make much sense when you think about it conceptually. Shouldn't a function be its own context and therefore have its own this? The reason why this is the case is not very complicated: JavaScript was originally created for novices to make scripting fast. So to make things easier, it auto-populates a function's this value with the global this or window.

That means window is available by default in all of your functions via this keyword. That's kind of useful, but it gets messy if you want a function to have a coherent, separated context.

Sloppy Mode

When we write JavaScript code, by default, all code is usually written in something called "sloppy mode," which accommodates for novices by ignoring some errors and causing functions to inherit the global context. To exit sloppy mode, we have to switch to something called "strict" mode.

Strict mode brings many advantages to your code, the main one being separating out function contexts from the global context. Both files and functions can be made strict by adding the "use strict" text at the top. By putting our code into strict mode, we can give each function its own context, and thus the keyword this will return undefined inside a function. In the following example, strict mode is enabled. To enable strict mode, you just have to add "use strict" to the top of your file:

```
"use strict"
console.log(this) // Window { }
let words = function (word1, word2) {
    console.log(this) // undefined
    return word1 + " " + word2
}
```

Arrow Notation Functionality with this

Now that we've looked at how different contexts work with functions, let's go back to arrow notation functions. Arrow functions are a little different from other functions in that they do not have their own context. That means that even in strict mode, they inherit it from their parents. This functionality only really makes sense in strict mode:

```
"use strict"
console.log(this) // Window { }
let words = () => {
    console.log(this)
}
words() // console logs Window { }
```

If your arrow function is inside another function, which is not using arrow notation, it inherits the context from that parent function. This can be seen in the following example:

```
"use strict"
let contextualFunction = function() {
    let words = () => {
        console.log(this) // console logs undefined
    }
    words()
}
contextualFunction() // console logs undefined
```

In general, strict mode is a more reliable way to write code. As well as that, it's pretty bad practice to expose global variables unknowingly to downstream scripts, which should perhaps not have access to them.

So far, while working in strict mode, this has been undefined inside functions. To make the this keyword more valuable, we will want to give it some kind of value. To do that, we need to understand the different ways we can call functions with context.

Calling Functions with Context

There are three methods inherited by all functions via prototypical inheritance, which allow us to call functions with a custom this context. These are listed below:

1. call(), which calls a function and gives it some context. Using call() can both define a context for a function and also pass variables to it (separated by commas).

2. apply(), which is the same as call() but uses an array to define the arguments of a function.

3. bind(), which permanently binds some context to a function – so you never have to redefine its context again.

call(). Suppose we want to define a constant value which is available within a specific function. We can achieve this functionality by adding our constant to the function's context

```
"use strict"
let words = function (word, punctuation) {
    return this.keyword + " " + word + punctuation
}
let wordContext = { keyword: "Hello" }
let helloWorld = words.call(wordContext, "World", "!")
console.log(helloWorld) // "Hello World!"
```

In this example, we pass the object wordContext into call() so that it becomes the context of the function and therefore its this value. Arguments are defined after the context and separated by commas – so "World" and "!" both become word and punctuation, respectively. You can see the output of this in Figure 6-3.

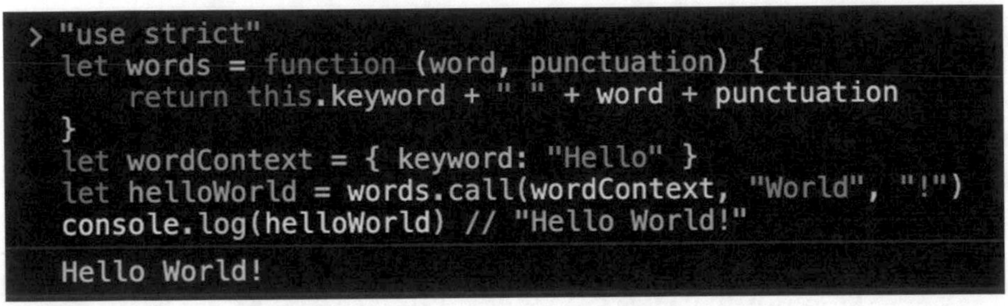

Figure 6-3. *Functions are added to the top of the stack as they are declared – just like variables*

Similar to the example above, apply() works in essentially the same way, with the only difference being that arguments are defined in an array. With apply, the code would look like this instead:

```
let helloWorld = words.apply(wordContext, [ "World", "!" ])
```

If we were calling words() all the time, we'll find that we will have to keep mentioning our context over and over again – which is not ideal. That's because we need to reference it every time we use call or apply. In the following example, we want to call words() twice and use the same context for each call. This means we have to write the same code twice:

```
"use strict"
let words = function (word, punctuation) {
    return this.keyword + " " + word + punctuation
}
let wordContext = {
    keyword: "Hello"
}
let helloWorld = words.call(wordContext, "World", "!")
let goodbye = words.call(wordContext, "Goodbye", "!")
console.log(helloWorld) // "Hello World!"
console.log(goodbye) // "Hello Goodbye!"
```

Although not a major problem, it does start to become an issue on large code bases. Instead, it's more efficient to use bind(). Using bind(), we only ever mention our context once, and then it permanently becomes entangled with our function. This can be seen in the following example:

```
"use strict"
let words = function (word, punctuation) {
    return this.keyword + " " + word + punctuation
}
let wordContext = {
    keyword: "Hello"
}
let boundWord = words.bind(wordContext)

let helloWorld = boundWord("World", "!")
let goodbye = boundWord("Goodbye", "!")
```

```
console.log(helloWorld) // "Hello World!"
console.log(goodbye) // "Hello Goodbye!"
```

Calling functions with context lends itself well to functional inheritance. Functions can inherit certain global variables or methods via context.

Constructor Functions in JavaScript

In the same way that we were able to make new instances of arrays and objects, we can use the new keyword to generate new instances of functions in JavaScript.

When you use the new keyword, it also has the added benefit of creating a new context – so your function will not inherit this from the global context. Due to this reason, you cannot use the new keyword with arrow notation functions then since they lack context.

Let's look at an example to familiarize ourselves with this concept. Functions called with new act much like functions which do not have new:

```
let myFunction = function(name, age, country) {
    console.log(this) // myFunction { }
}

let newFunction = new myFunction("John", 24, "Britain")
```

Note   With the new keyword, you can omit the double brackets when calling your function if you have no arguments. So new myFunction() is the same as new myFunction.

Since they generate their own context, console logging of this will return myFunction { }, which contains details about the function (under constructor), and the global prototype for object types since functions are of type object. You can see what this looks like in Figure 6-4.

```
▼ myFunction {} ℹ
  ▼ [[Prototype]]: Object
    ▼ constructor: f (name, age, country)
        arguments: null
        caller: null
        length: 3
        name: "myFunction"
      ▶ prototype: {constructor: f}
        [[FunctionLocation]]: VM1463:1
      ▶ [[Prototype]]: f ()
      ▶ [[Scopes]]: Scopes[2]
    ▶ [[Prototype]]: Object
```

Figure 6-4. When using the new keyword, this refers to the function's prototype, which contains details on the function, and its inherited object prototype. This is not super important for writing code from day to day but is useful to know nonetheless

Creating encapsulated functions which have their own context turns out to be quite useful. For example, we can assign details passed in the argument of our function to our this context like so:

```
let myFunction = function(name, age, country) {
    this.assignedName = name
    this.assignedAge = age
    this.assignedCountry = country
    console.log(this) // Contains assignedAge, assignedCountry,
    and assignedName
}
```

```
let newFunction = new myFunction("John", 24, "Britain")
console.log(newFunction) // Contains assignedAge,
assignedCountry, and assignedName
```

Every time we call a new instance of our function, we create a new context, and the function is self-contained. While this seems similar to creating an object containing new values, it gives us the added value of being able to manipulate or change assigned values.

For example, suppose we are building an application that allows user registration. We could create a constructor function which, when called, is different for each user, as shown in the following example:

```
let User = function(firstName, lastName, age) {
    this.fullName = firstName + " " + lastName
    this.age = age
}
```

```
let userOne = new User("John", "Big", 24)
console.log(userOne) // { fullName: "John Big", age: 24 }
```

```
let userTwo = new User("John", "Small", 24)
console.log(userTwo) // { fullName: "John Small", age: 24 }
```

It is also possible to check if functions were constructed with new if you need to. Although not a best practice, it can give you context in some edge-case scenarios. You can do this by checking new.target, which when undefined, means that the function was called without new:

```
let User = function(firstName, lastName, age) {
    if(new.target) {
        this.fullName = firstName + " " + lastName
        this.age = age
    }
```

```
    else {
        return "Hello World"
    }
}

let userOne = new User("John", "Big", 24)
console.log(userOne) // { fullName: "John Big", age: 24 }

let userTwo = User("John", "Small", 24)
console.log(userTwo) // "Hello World"
```

Additional Function Methods

This way of writing code is object-oriented. The user is the object, in this case, and we can then define that a "user" can do certain things. We can attach the methods that a user can do to the User function itself. The User function, known as a constructor, then lets us construct a user, who can do multiple things. To illustrate this, let's try adding a method to our function. For example, let's allow a user can give their name:

```
let User = function(firstName, lastName, age) {
    this.fullName = firstName + " " + lastName
    this.age = age
}

User.prototype.giveName = function() {
    return `My name is ${this.fullName}!`
}
```

Since fullName is already defined by the constructor function, it will be available in User.prototype.name. Then, when we want the user to give their name, we only have to call the function userOne.giveName():

```
let userOne = new User("John", "Big", 24)

// Console logs "My name is John Big!"
console.log(userOne.giveName())
```

Getters and Setters

As well as all of the regular function expressions we've looked at so far, special functions can be defined inside objects known as getters and setters. As the name suggests, they let us get or set values on an object. Getters and setters are just syntactic sugar – they make your code a little easier to understand from the outside, but their functionality can be achieved with standalone functions too.

Consider this example, where we store animal names on our object. Here, we have one get function – to get the "value" property of our object and a set method to add new animals to that value property. Inside an object, this refers to the object itself. This is also true for normal functions set inside of objects:

```
let Animals = {
    value: [ 'dog', 'cat' ],
    get listAnimals() {
        return this.value
    },
    set newAnimal(name) {
        this.value.push(name)
        console.log("New animal added: " + name)
    }
}
Animals.newAnimal = "sheep"
console.log(Animals.listAnimals)
```

What is interesting about getters and setters is that you don't call them using the double brackets like `Animals.newAnimal()`. Instead, they are called whenever you check the property name. So `Animals.newAnimal` = "sheep" is used rather than `Animals.newAnimal("sheep")`. Similarly, `Animals.listAnimals` will list all animals, without needing to run the function.

This gives them the appearance of being normal properties, with the added benefit of being able to run functional code.

Generator Functions

The final type of function we'll look at is known as the generator function. Earlier, when we looked at array iteration, we mentioned how we could create an iterator with access to the `next()` method by accessing the iterator protocol:

```
let myArray = [ "lightning", "apple", "squid", "speaker" ]
let getIterator = myArray[Symbol.iterator]()
console.log(getIterator.next()) // {value: 'lightning',
done: false}
```

Generator functions work in a similar way and are denoted by `function*`. A simple generator function looks like this:

```
function* someGenerator(x) {
    yield x;
}
const runG = generator(1)
console.log(runG.next()) // {value: 1, done: false}
console.log(runG.next()) // {value: undefined, done: true}
```

Every time you use `yield` in a generator function, it represents a stopping point for `next()`. You can think of `yield` as the generator function version of `return`. Since we only used `yield` once in this function, `next()`

will only work once. After that, it will be marked as done as is shown in the previous example. As such, generator functions remember where you left off and continue on from that point.

In the following example, we run an infinite loop, which also increases the value of a variable called index each time. The function remembers the value of index, each time we run next, allowing us to access the next calculation in the sequence each time:

```
function* someGenerator(x) {
    let index = 0
    while(true) {
        yield x * 10 * index
        ++index
    }
}
```

```
const runG = someGenerator(5)
console.log(runG.next()) // {value: 0, done: false}
console.log(runG.next()) // {value: 50, done: false}
console.log(runG.next()) // {value: 100, done: false}
console.log(runG.next()) // {value: 150, done: false}
```

If we try to use return in a generator function, the "done" state will be set to true and the generator will stop working:

```
function* someGenerator(x) {
    let index = 0
    while(true) {
        yield x * 10 * index
        return 5
    }
}
```

```
const runG = someGenerator(5)
console.log(runG.next()) // {value: 0, done: false}
console.log(runG.next()) // {value: 5, done: true}
console.log(runG.next()) // {value: undefined, done: true}
```

If you need to use another generator function within a generator function, you can defer yield to that new generator function instead. In those scenarios, we use yield*. For example, yield* myFunc() would take the yield value from myFunc() and use it in the current function.

Classes

JavaScript is a prototypical language, and as we've seen already, inheritance occurs via prototypes. Many other languages have classes, which can make JavaScript seem like quite a departure in syntax.

To alleviate this problem of unfamiliarity, JavaScript implemented classes. For the most part though, classes in JavaScript are basically just syntactic sugar for writing constructor functions, with a few additional capabilities specific to classes.

Classes do not have to be used to write JavaScript since they provide little in the way of new functionality, but they are becoming more common as JavaScript inherits more developers who are used to writing class based software. Classes always have to be called with the new keyword, and they always run in strict mode, so they create their own context by default without the need of strict mode.

Classes and Constructor Functions

Classes can have a constructor function, which is the function that runs any time they are called, but they don't need to have one. In classes, constructor functions are defined using the constructor keyword, and you can only have one constructor function per class. They behave like normal functions, and any arguments passed to the class will go into the constructor function, as is shown in the following example:

```
let myClass = class {
    constructor(name) {
        console.log(name)
    }
}
new myClass("hello") // Console logs "hello"
```

For context, this example is the equivalent of writing the following functional code:

```
let myFunction = function(name) {
    console.log(name)
}
new myFunction("hello") // Console logs "hello"
```

Classes can be written in two ways, either where we use a let or const variable to define the class:

```
let myClass = class { // ...
```

Or using the class keyword followed by the class name:

```
class myClass { // ...
```

Class Methods

Just like when we declare functions using the new keyword, we can also define methods on classes. These are defined directly in the class body and work in the same way. As an example of how this works in practice, let's create a class called HotSauce, with a couple properties and a method to retrieve how hot the sauce is.

There are a few things worth noting here:

1. At the top level of the class body, variables can be defined within a class without variable keywords. That's because they act like the properties of an object. Variables at the top level of the class join the class's context. In this example, I assign units and maxHotness to the context of the class, so can be accessed via this in methods.

2. Methods are written like method() instead of function method().

3. Classes don't have arguments, but you can call a class with arguments. The arguments on the constructor are where the arguments used on the class are passed to.

4. Classes ultimately create objects, just like functions. If you try console logging new HotSauce('Chilli Wave', 4600), you'll get an object back, as shown in Figure 6-5.

5. Finally, arguments passed to a class are not available by default to the entire class. As such, it's pretty common to see code that takes arguments from the constructor function and assigns them to this. That's what we do in the following for the name and hotness of the hot sauce defined:

```
let HotSauce = class {
    // Fields here are added to this, so they are
        available
    // via this.units and this.maxHotness in methods
    units = 'scoville'
    maxHotness = 20000000
```

119

```
    constructor(name, hotness) {
        // We can assign arguments from new
            instances of
        // our class to this as well
        this.hotness = hotness
        this.name = name
    }
    getName() {
        if(this.hotness < this.maxHotness) {
            return `${this.name} is ${this.hotness}
            ${this.units}`
        }
        else {
            return `${this.name} is too hot!`
        }
    }
}

let newSauce = new HotSauce('Chilli Wave', 4600)
// Console logs 'Chilli Wave is 4600 scoville
scovilles'
console.log(newSauce.getName())
```

```
▼ HotSauce {units: 'scoville', max
    hotness: 4600
    maxHotness: 20000000
    name: "Chilli Wave"
    units: "scoville"
  ▼ [[Prototype]]: Object
    ▶ constructor: class
    ▶ getName: ƒ getName()
    ▶ [[Prototype]]: Object
```

Figure 6-5. *Classes create objects. If we log the instance we created of our HotSauce class, newSauce, we'll get an object containing all the properties we defined, along with a prototype containing our methods*

Class Method Types

By default, all class methods are public. That means they can be changed outside of the class. They will also show up in the console log and can even be deleted. For example, we could totally rewrite our getName method if we wanted to, outside of the class:

```
let newSauce = new HotSauce('Chilli Wave', 4600)
newSauce.getName = function() {
    return "No Hot Sauce for you!"
}
// No Hot Sauce for you!
console.log(newSauce.getName())
```

Sometimes, you don't want a class editable like this. As such, JavaScript provides two other types of fields we can use with classes:

- **Static fields**, which cannot be accessed on a new instance of a class itself but only on the original class (which we'll look at in more detail soon)

- **Private fields**, which can only be accessed from within the class itself

121

Static Method Fields

Static methods and fields are usually used for utility functions. Consider this class, where a simple static method will return some details on the class:

```
let Utility = class {
    static className = "Utility Functions"
    static author = "Some Author"

    static classDetails() {
        return `${this.className} by ${this.author}`
    }
}
```

If we try to initialize this class and call `classDetails()`, we'll receive a type error since classDetails cannot be called on a new instance of Utility.

```
let callUtility = new Utility
console.log(callUtility.classDetails())
```

Instead, we need to call the static method directly on the `Utility` class as is shown in the following example:

```
// Utility Functions by Some Author
console.log(Utility.classDetails())
```

Since we don't initiate a new instance of our class, `static` methods will also not have access to non-static properties on the class. For example, if we had not called `className` and author static in the preceding example, then they would have been `undefined` when we tried to reference them in `classDetails()`.

Just like their public counterparts, static methods can be deleted or changed on the class itself. For example, we could redefine classDetails() to something completely different:

```
Utility.classDetails = function() {
    return "Some return text"
}
```

Static methods can also be getters and setters. If we changed our classDetails() function from static classDetails() to static get classDetails(), we could then call it as Utility.classDetails. The same applies to setters.

Finally, we can create static initializers to run upon class initialization. This lets us run some functionality when calling static properties or methods even though static methods cannot accept arguments. In the following example, we update the author static variable to "Hello World" upon class initialization:

```
let Utility = class {
    static className = "Utility Functions"
    static author = "Some Author"
    static {
        this.author =  "Hello World"
    }
    static classDetails() {
        return `${this.className} by ${this.author}`
    }
}

Utility.classDetails() // Utility Functions by Hello World
```

Private Method Fields

Private method fields are not available outside of the class itself. While constructors in classes cannot be private, everything else can be. The following example shows a private field defined inside a class. Private fields are defined with a hash at the start:

```
let myClass = class {
    #privateField = 1
}

let newClass = new myClass()
```

If we try console logging newClass, privateField will not be available. Furthermore, trying to refer to newClass.#privateField will throw a syntax error.

Note   While private fields will throw errors in code if referred to outside of a class, they may show in the console in some browsers. That is because it can be useful in console logs and debugging to be able to access these fields.

While all the other features of classes are just features objects already had, private fields are actually new functionality that are only available via classes. Private fields are not available on objects in the same way as they are in classes.

Class Inheritance via Extends

Since classes are mostly syntactic sugar on top of objects, they also have typical prototypical inheritance too. If you create a new class which extends another class, the class which extends will simply become the prototype of the child class. Consider the following example, using our HotSauce class:

```
class HotSauce {
    // Fields here are added to this, so they are available
    // via this.units and this.maxHotness in methods
    units = 'scoville'
    maxHotness = 20000000

    constructor(name, hotness) {
        // We can assign arguments from new instances of
        // our class to this as well
        this.hotness = hotness
        this.name = name
    }
    getName() {
        if(this.hotness < this.maxHotness) {
            return `${this.name} is ${this.hotness}
            ${this.units}`
        }
        else {
            return `${this.name} is too hot!`
        }
    }
}
```

From Figure 6-5, you'll see that the prototype of this class contains the methods getName() and the constructor. To further explain this concept, let's create a new class which extends this, called VeganHotSauce. This logically makes sense since only some hot sauces are vegan:

```
class VeganHotSauce extends HotSauce {
    constructor(meat, name, hotness) {
        super(name, hotness)
```

```
        this.meat = meat
    }

    checkMeatContent() {
        if(this.meat) {
            return "this is not vegan"
        }
        else {
            return "no meat detected"
        }
    }
}

let newVeganOption = new VeganHotSauce(false, "Vegan
Lite", 2400)
console.log(newVeganOption)
```

There are a few things going on here worth noting:

- We're introducing the super() function for the first time. This is a special function which calls the parent class, along with its constructor. Here, this is the same as running new HotSauce(name, hotness). Essentially, this means we're running the HotSauce constructor anytime VeganHotSauce is run, while also setting this.meat to the meat variable from VeganHotSauce.

- Using this keyword, our new constructor for VeganHotSauce can pass arguments to the parent class. Here, we can pass the name and hotness.

- The outcome of running this class, which can be seen in Figure 6-6.

```
  VeganHotSauce {units: 'scoville', maxHotnes
▼ t: false} ⓘ
    hotness: 2400
    maxHotness: 20000000
    meat: false
    name: "Vegan Lite"
    units: "scoville"
  ▼ [[Prototype]]: HotSauce
    ▶ checkMeatContent: ƒ checkMeatContent()
    ▶ constructor: class VeganHotSauce
    ▼ [[Prototype]]: Object
      ▶ constructor: class HotSauce
      ▶ getName: ƒ getName()
      ▶ [[Prototype]]: Object
```

Figure 6-6. *VeganHotSauce contains all the top-level properties from HotSauce at the top level too. Methods for VeganHotSauce are contained within its prototype, and methods from HotSauce are in its prototype's prototype*

As you might expect, both static and private methods are not inherited when using extends. That is because both, conceptually, belong to the parent class.

Class Inheritance Super Keyword

We used the super keyword in the VeganHotSauce example to call its parent class. The super keyword is special in JavaScript since it behaves differently depending on where you put it. If you put super in a constructor for an extended class, it can be used as a function – so super(... arguments) is completely valid.

Meanwhile, outside of constructors, you can only use super in the form super[field] or super.field to call upon parent properties. In fact, if you try to call it as a function outside of the constructor, an error will be thrown. That means in a class's methods, we can use super only to reference properties of the parent class. So for example, if we wanted to use our parents method, getName(), in our child class VeganHotSauce, then we'd call super.getName():

```
class VeganHotSauce extends HotSauce {
    constructor(meat, name, hotness) {
        super(name, hotness)
        this.meat = meat
    }

    checkMeatContent() {

        console.log()
        if(this.meat) {
            return "this is not vegan.. but " + super.getName()
        }
        else {
            return "no meat detected.. and " + super.getName()
        }
    }
}

let newVeganOption = new VeganHotSauce(false, "Vegan
Lite", 2400)
// console logs
// no meat detected.. and Vegan Lite is 2400 scovilles
console.log(newVeganOption.checkMeatContent())
```

It is worth noting that while we can call super.getName(), we can't call super.units – and that's because units are not on the prototype of VeganHotSauce. Take a look at Figure 6-6 again, and you'll see why.

Even though units is a parent property, when inherited it appears on the VeganHotSauce class instead. The super keyword is used to access prototype methods and properties from the parent class. If we want to access units, we have to use this.units rather than super.units.

Summary

In this chapter, we've covered quite a lot of ground on functions and classes. We've shown you how to create functions and how they inherit based on prototypical inheritance. We've talked about how to give functions context with the this keyword. We've also looked at the many different ways you can define functions in your code, and how they differ. Finally, we've looked at classes, and explained how they are mostly syntactic sugar for objects. We've gone into detail using examples on how class inheritance work in JavaScript. While classes can be familiar to some developers, if you find it hard to understand or unintuitive, it's still fine to just work with functions and prototypical inheritance where necessary.

Whether you decide to use classes or functions is mostly stylistic. In JavaScript, many developers use functions since that's the way the language was originally devised. As mentioned before, the most important thing is that you maintain consistency in your code and that your team understand what the code you are writing means.

CHAPTER 7

Types

In software development, a type refers to a property we apply to a language construct to describe what the data is about. In this description, a language construct refers to something like an expression or variable. We've already discussed how JavaScript is both weakly and dynamically typed, which means we do not have to explicitly declare types on language constructs. That does not, however, make types in JavaScript any more straightforward than other languages, and in some ways, it makes things more complicated! Types are where some of the more unusual quirks of JavaScript come to roost, so getting a good grasp on them can be tricky.

Since we will be talking about types in this chapter, it's useful to understand how to find the type of something. The type of anything can be found using the typeof keyword:

```
console.log(typeof 5) // 'number'
console.log(typeof "name") // 'string'
```

Primitive Types

Primitive types are types which have no methods or properties by default, and are not objects. These types of data cannot be changed once they are defined, and in memory terms are stored on the stack. In JavaScript, there are a total of 7 primitive types, all of which are all listed in Table 7-1. We've seen some of these types already in our code.

Table 7-1. *JavaScript primitive types*

Operators	Definition
number	Any numeric value
	For example:
	`let x = 5`
string	Any string value
	For example:
	`let x = "Hello World"`
bigint	Any integer which is defined as bigint (has an n after the integer). Used for creating safe integers beyond the maximum safe integer limit
	For example:
	`let x = 1000n`
undefined	Any undefined data (i.e., a variable with no value)
	For example:
	`let x = undefined`
boolean	Any true or false value
	For example:
	`let x = true`
null	A reference that points to a nonexistent address in memory
	For example:
	`let x = null`
symbol	A guaranteed unique identifier
	For example:
	`let x = Symbol("id")`

Note   null is not an object, but typeof null returns object as its type. This is a long-standing bug in JavaScript, but it cannot be fixed because it would break too many code bases.

Primitive Wrappers

By definition, primitives have no methods, but they often behave as though they do. Every primitive type except for null and undefined are associated with what are known as wrapper objects, which are referenced every time you try to call a method on a primitive type. As an example, the wrapper object for string types is called String. You can find all the methods you can apply to strings by console logging String.prototype, which can be seen in Figure 7-1.

```
> console.log(String.prototype)
  ▼ String {'', constructor: ƒ, anchor:
    ▶ anchor: ƒ anchor()
    ▶ at: ƒ at()
    ▶ big: ƒ big()
    ▶ blink: ƒ blink()
    ▶ bold: ƒ bold()
    ▶ charAt: ƒ charAt()
    ▶ charCodeAt: ƒ charCodeAt()
    ▶ codePointAt: ƒ codePointAt()
    ▶ concat: ƒ concat()
    ▶ constructor: ƒ String()
    ▶ endsWith: ƒ endsWith()
    ▶ fixed: ƒ fixed()
    ▶ fontcolor: ƒ fontcolor()
```

Figure 7-1. *Console logging the prototype of a wrapper object like* String *will give you all the methods that can be applied to that type.* *All the preceding methods can be applied directly to any string*

The wrapper objects for common JavaScript types are as follows:

- Object

- Symbol

- Number

- String

- BigInt

- Boolean

If you ever need to know what methods are available to various types, you can find them by console logging `Wrapper.prototype`, where `Wrapper` is `Object`, `Symbol`, `Number`, etc.

Calling methods from a wrapper on a primitive type can be done directly on the primitive itself or on a variable pointing to the primitive. In the following example, we use one of those methods, `.at()`, on a string and on a variable of type string:

```
let someVariable = 'string'
someVariable.at(1) // 't'
'string'.at(2) // 'r'
```

This applies to all types, so the methods found on `Object.prototype` can be applied directly to any `Object`. The only slight quirk to this is that if you want to apply a number method to a `Number` type, you have to wrap the number in brackets. This might seem strange, but it's because the dot after a number is interpreted as a decimal point, not the start of a new method. You can also call number methods on a number by using two dots, where the first dot is the decimal, and the second refers to the method. This can be seen in the following example:

```
(5).toString() // '5'
5..toString() // '5'
```

Number methods can also be called via Number.toString().

```
Number.toString(5) // '5'
```

Another thing worth noting is that primitive wrappers can sometimes define static methods and properties that can be called directly on the wrapper itself. We covered static methods in a previous chapter on functions.

MAX_SAFE_INTEGER is found on the Number wrapper object, so calling Number.MAX_SAFE_INTEGER gives the maximum safe integer that can be used in JavaScript. You can see this in action in Figure 7-2.

```
> console.log(Number.MAX_SAFE_INTEGER)
  9007199254740991
```

Figure 7-2. *Some wrapper objects have static properties and methods which can come in useful when coding. Here is the max safe integer, found on the Number wrapper*

As another example, the static method keys() can be found on the Object wrapper, and can be called to get the keys of any Object:

```
Object.keys({ "hello" : "world", "goodbye" : "world" })
// [ "hello", "goodbye" ]
```

To summarize what we've discussed so far:

1. A number of primitive types exist in JavaScript which have no methods or properties by default. They are also immutable. These are things like string, number, and boolean.

2. All types in JavaScript, including primitives and objects, inherit methods from wrapper objects. So all data of type string will inherit all the methods found on String.prototype.

3. If you need to find out what methods you can use on any type of data in JavaScript, you could google it... or you could `console.log` the wrapper prototype to see them all like `console.log(String.prototype)`.

4. Methods found on the top level of a wrapper object's prototype (i.e., `String.prototype.at()`) can be called directly on anything of that type – for example, `'string'.at(2)`.

5. Static methods exist on most wrapper objects. These are usually found in a constructor function of that wrapper, that is, `Number.constructor.MAX_SAFE_INTEGER`, and they must be called via the wrapper object – like `Object.keys()`, or `Object.values()`.

Using Wrappers to Create Types

Wrappers can be used to create new data of a certain type. For example, a new string can be created like so, with the added benefit of also coercing other types to the strings:

```
let newString = String("hello") // "hello"
let objString = String({ "some" : "object" }) // "[object
Object]"
let newString = String(5) // "5"
```

The same works for numbers, which coerces numerical strings into numbers:

```
let newNumber = Number("5") // 5
```

While calling Number() and String() like this creates a new primitive, calling it as a classic constructor with the new keyword will lead to some unexpected behavior. For example, new String will create an object without an accessible primitive value:

```
let newString = new String("hello") // String { "hello" }
let newNumber = new Number(5) // Number { 5 }
```

The behavior of using these primitive wrappers as constructors is quite unreliable, so it's generally recommended you avoid this. Newer types aren't even compatible with the new keyword – so new Symbol() and new BigInt() both throw type errors.

The Number Type and NaN

We've already spoken about null and undefined, which represent something with no value or something which is undefined. Another value, NaN, can also appear in your code if you try to create a number out of something that is clearly not a number. An example of how you would achieve this is by wrapping it in Number(), like we did earlier, or by using a method to coerce it to an object like parseFloat() or parseInt():

```
parseInt("5") // the Number 5
parseInt({ "key" : "value" }) // NaN
```

Parsing an object or something that is not easily coerced to a number returns NaN or "Not a Number." NaN is a global property. NaN has some weird behavior. It is the only value in JavaScript that does not equal itself, for example:

```
NaN === NaN // false
5 === 5 // true
```

The reason NaN behaves this way is defined in a specification called IEEE 754. In a way, having NaN not equal itself makes some sense. If it did, then NaN/NaN would equal 1, which would be a number. While it may seem logical to assume that it does not equal itself because it's an object with a different reference, NaN is not an object.In fact, even though NaN means "Not a Number," it's of type number if you check:

```
typeof NaN // "number"
```

The confusion does not stop there. Since we can't check if something is NaN by doing NaN === NaN, we have a function called isNaN to do the job instead:

```
isNaN(5) // false
isNaN(NaN) // true
```

If something is NaN, this function returns true. If something is of type number, it will tell you if it's NaN or not. If something is another type, it will coerce that data to a number and then tell you if it's a number – and some of those conversions are unexpected.

For example, boolean values like true and false become 1 and 0. So isNaN(false) and isNaN(true) both return false even though true and false are not numbers. An empty string will also be parsed as false and therefore turn into 0, meaning it will also return false. Arrays of one number also become number types. This makes isNaN relatively unreliable for checking if something is a number or not:

```
isNaN(" ") // false
isNaN(NaN) // true
isNaN(false) // false
isNaN([5]) // false
```

To fix this, JavaScript added a new method later on, which does not coerce data into numbers if it wasn't a number in the first place. The name of that method is the same, but it's found via `Number.isNaN()`, instead of `isNaN()` (or `window.isNaN()`). This is, to say the least, a little confusing.

So while `isNaN("hello")` is false since `Number("hello")` converts to NaN, `Number.isNaN("hello")` is false since `"hello"` is not equal to "NaN." As such, `Number.isNaN` is a much more reliable way to check if something is NaN since no type coercion is involved – but it only checks for direct equality to NaN itself.

In summary:

- `isNaN()` coerces types to numbers. For example, `isNaN("hello")` will perform `Number("hello")` which results in NaN, and this will return true.

- `Number.isNaN()` will not coerce types to numbers. It will return false when asked `Number.isNaN("hello")` since "hello" does not equal NaN.

Number Type Mathematics

Number types do contain some constants relating to JavaScript itself, like `Number.MAX_SAFE_INTEGER`, but the Number wrapper object does not contain mathematical constants, which are extremely useful when working with Number types. Instead, JavaScript has another global object called Math, which contains these properties along with some useful methods. A list of all mathematical constants can be found in Table 7-2.

Table 7-2. *Mathematical constants in JavaScript*

Mathematical Constant	What It Returns	Value (to 3dp)
Math.PI	Returns PI	3.141 ...
Math.E	Returns Euler's number	2.718 ...
Math.E	Returns Euler's number	2.718 ...
Math.LN2	Returns ln(2)	0.693 ...
Math.LOG10E	Returns log10(e)	0.434 ...
Math.LOG2E	Returns log2(e)	1.442 ...
Math.LN10	Returns ln(10)	2.302 ...
Math.SQRT2	Returns the square root of 2	1.414 ...
Math.SQRT1_2	Returns the square root of 1/2	0.707 ...

These mathematical constants can be used in any mathematical equation, using standard mathematical notation. For example:

```
let x = 5 * Math.PI // 5 times Pi
let y = 10 * Math.E // 10 times e
```

We've covered many mathematical operations in other examples throughout the book. To ensure we've covered everything, here is the full list, along with their definition. All of these can be applied to Number types:

1. + (plus) – Adds two numbers together, that is,
    `let x = 10 + 5` returns 15

2. – (minus) – Subtracts one number from another,
    that is, `let x = 10 - 5` returns 5

3. / (divide) – Divides one number by another, that is,
    `let x = 10 / 2` returns 5

4. * (multiply) – Multiplies two numbers together, that
    is, `let x = 10 * 10` returns 100

5. % (remainder) – Gets the remainder when dividing
    one number by another, that is, `let x = 12 % 5`
    returns 2 since the remainder of 12 / 5 is 2

6. ** Raises one number to the power of another, that
    is, `let x = 5 ** 2` returns 25 as it raises 5 to the
    power of two (5 squared)

Mathematical Methods

As we've mentioned, number types not only have the wrapper type
`Number` but also a utility global object called `Math` that contains a bunch
of mathematical constants and methods. While we've looked at the
constants already, the methods that exist on this global object are also
quite useful. It's worth familiarizing yourself with some of these. You can
see some of these in Figure 7-3.

```
> console.log(Math)
  ▼ Math {abs: f, acos: f, acosh: f, asin: f, asinh: f, …} ⓘ
      E: 2.718281828459045
      LN2: 0.6931471805599453
      LN10: 2.302585092994046
      LOG2E: 1.4426950408889634
      LOG10E: 0.4342944819032518
      PI: 3.141592653589793
      SQRT1_2: 0.7071067811865476
      SQRT2: 1.4142135623730951
    ▶ abs: ƒ abs()
    ▶ acos: ƒ acos()
    ▶ acosh: ƒ acosh()
    ▶ asin: ƒ asin()
```

*Figure 7-3. If in doubt about an object, always console log it! Console
logging Math (which can be done from your browser's console log)
shows you all the mathematical constants and methods you can use*

Some particular useful mathematical methods found on the math global object include the following:

- `Math.abs(number)` – Returns the absolute or magnitude of a number (removes minus sign). So `Math.abs(-2)` returns 2.

- `Math.sign(number)` – Returns the sign of a number. So `Math.sign(-144)` returns -1, and `Math.sign(4953)` returns 1.

- `Math.floor(number)` – Rounds down a number, so `Math.floor(2.78764)` returns 2.

- `Math.ceil(number)` – Rounds up a number, so `Math.ceil(2.2344)` returns 3.

- `Math.round(number)` – Rounds a number as per normal rounding rules. So `Math.round(2.5)` returns 3, and `Math.round(2.2)` returns 2.

- `Math.max(number, number, …)` – Returns the max number from a set. So `Math.max(4, 10, 15, 18)` returns 18.

- `Math.min(number, number, …)` – The same as `Math.max` but returns the lowest value number.

- `Math.trunc(number)` – Returns only the integer part of a number. So `Math.trunc(14.5819)` returns 14.

- `Math.sqrt(number)` – Square roots a number.

- `Math.cbrt(number)` – Cube roots a number.

- `Math.random()` – Returns a random number between 0 and 1.

- `Math.pow(number, power)` – Returns a number raised to a power. So `Math.pow(2, 5)` returns 32.

As well as these there are `log` methods, which are listed in the following, and all geometric methods you would expect, like `Math.tan`, `Math.sin`, `Math.atanh`, `Math.asin`, and so on:

- `Math.log(number)` for the natural log of a number

- `Math.log2(number)` for the base 2 log of a number

- `Math.log10(number)` for the base 10 log a number

- `Math.log1p(number)` for the natural log of the number plus 1

All of these methods are useful for manipulating number types. To summarize what we've learned about Number types in this section:

1. Number types have static methods assigned to them via the Number wrapper. The Number wrapper also contains some JavaScript constants relating to numbers.

2. A special value called NaN or "Not a Number" exists in JavaScript. It signifies something which is not a number. It has some quirks (as we've explored) and a few utility methods like `isNaN()` and `Number.isNaN()`.

3. Number types also have a utility objcct called `Math`, which contains mathematical constants and useful mathematical static methods.

The Date Type

One glaring omission which you may have already noticed is the lack of a specific primitive "`Date`" type in JavaScript, unlike in other languages. While variables and expressions cannot be given the type "date", there is a wrapper object called Date, which helps us manipulate dates. Declaring the `Date` object returns a string of the current date, which you can see in Figure 7-4.

```
let currentDate = Date() // The current date
```

```
> console.log(Date())
  Thu Sep 07 2023 20:41:09 GMT+0100 (British Summer Time)
```

Figure 7-4. *Calling the Date() constructor will create a string of the current date and time*

Unlike the other wrapper objects we've looked at, it's actually better to call Date as a constructor since you get a bunch of useful utility methods along with it:

```
let currentDate = new Date() // Date Object
```

Dates in JavaScript are notoriously quirky, and most of the strangeness is down to the fact that a date in JavaScript is actually a date time. Under the hood, the dates which are returned by Date are actually unix timestamp – but in milliseconds, instead of seconds. That means that for day to day purposes, you usually need to divide this number by 1000 from the get-go, for it to be useful.

Once you have created a date, you can then use utility methods, like getTime(), to convert this to the unix timestamp in milliseconds:

```
let date = new Date().getTime()
```

```
// Console logs the current timestamp.
console.log(date);
// i.e. 1625858618210
```

The various methods for getting dates in JavaScript are shown below:

- new Date().getDay() – Gets the day of the week counting from 0 and starting on Sunday, so Friday would be 5.

- `new Date().getDate()` – Gets the date of the month, so the 9th July would return 9.

- `new Date().getMonth()` – Gets the number of the current month counting from 0, so the 9th July would return 6.

- `new Date().getFullYear()` – Gets the number of the current year, that is, 2021.

- `new Date().getSeconds()` – Gets the current seconds count.

- `new Date().getMilliseconds()` – Gets the milliseconds count (from 0 to 999).

- `new Date().getMinutes()` – Gets the current minutes count.

- `new Date().getHours()` – Gets the current hours count.

- `new Date().getTimezoneOffset()` – Gets the time zone offset from 0, counted in minutes.

- `new Date().toISOString()` – Gets the date and time in the ISO 8061 standard.

It's also worth noting that JavaScript's Date() constructor can parse date strings into dates, but since this behavior is not standardized across browsers, it's generally not recommended:

```
let newDate = new Date("2023-01-01")
console.log(newDate) // Gives Jan 1st 2023
```

If you need to parse a date, it's better to pass in the year, month, and day separately – to ensure it works in all browsers:

```
let newDate = new Date("2023", "01", "01")
```

Alternatively, all the preceding get methods when changed to set allow you to set a date. For example, getDate() becomes setDate(), to set the day of the month; getFullYear() becomes setFullYear(), and so on:

```
let newDate = new Date()
newDate.setFullYear("1993")
newDate.setDate("5")
newDate.setMonth("5")
console.log(newDate) // 5th June 1993
```

Dates can be converted to locale strings which are formatted in a more user-friendly form. This configuration, while not the most flexible thing in the world, can allow you to put dates into a more recognizable format. The .toLocaleString() function accepts both a locale code and a configuration object defining how the weekday, year, month, day, hour, minute, and second should be defined. An example of this is shown in the following:

```
let date = new Date()
let localOptions = { weekday: 'long', year: 'numeric', month:
'long', day: 'numeric', hour: 'numeric', 'minute' : 'numeric' }

let inFrench = date.toLocaleString('fr-FR', localOptions);

// Returns vendredi 9 juillet 2021, 21:53
console.log(inFrench)
```

The locality defined here is fr-FR, but en-GB or en-US would also be valid. The two-digit language comes first, followed by a dash, and then the two-digit country code. These codes follow ISO 3166 and ISO 639, respectively.

We used toLocaleString() earlier, but toLocaleDateString() and toLocaleTimeString() can also be used. The difference is one returns the date while the other returns just the time.

The Symbol Type

In a previous chapter on iteration, we covered how we can access step-by-step iteration via the iteration protocol found on any iterable type, like arrays. To access this iteration, we used a key on all arrays called "Symbol. iterator":

```
let myArray = [ "apple", "squid", "speaker" ]
let getIterator = myArray[Symbol.iterator]()
console.log(getIterator)
```

This iterator property utilises symbols. Symbols are special primitives which always guarantee a unique value. They are quite useful in objects where keys may be introduced that could conflict with existing ones.

Imagine, for example, you had a specific property on an object called "id," which you did not want changed. With normal property keys, this can happen quite easily:

```
let myObject = { "id" : "some-id" }
myObject.id = "some-other-id"
```

This can be avoided with symbols. In the following example, we create a new symbol for "id," and try to create another key on the object using a symbol for "id" again. Even though Symbol("id") === Symbol("id") may seem like it should be true, they will both refer to different things. As such we can access both keys independently. You can see the output of this code in Figure 7-5.

```
let idSymbol1 = Symbol("id")
let idSymbol2 = Symbol("id")

let myObject = { [idSymbol1]: "some-id", [idSymbol2] :
"some-other-id" }

console.log(myObject[idSymbol1]) // "some-id"
console.log(myObject[idSymbol2]) // "some-other-id"
```

```
> let idSymbol1 = Symbol("id")
  let idSymbol2 = Symbol("id")

  let myObject = { [idSymbol1]: "some-id", [idSymbol2] : "some-other-id" }

  console.log(myObject)
  console.log(myObject[idSymbol1]) // "some-id"
  console.log(myObject[idSymbol2]) // "some-other-id"

  ▶ {Symbol(id): 'some-id', Symbol(id): 'some-other-id'}

  some-id

  some-other-id
```

Figure 7-5. *Symbols allow for the creation of unique keys which are unique regardless of their name, allowing you to avoid key conflicts when adding new items to objects*

While the preceding code has allowed us to create unique values using the Symbol constructor, you can still create unique keys with symbols that do override each other. Symbol.for() will find a symbol for a specific key or create one if it is not found. This will mean that you can only create one symbol "for" a specific key. In our previous example, this would allow the keys to override each other:

```
let idSymbol1 = Symbol.for("id")
let idSymbol2 = Symbol.for("id")

let myObject = { [idSymbol1]: "some-id", [idSymbol2] :
"some-other-id" }

console.log(myObject[idSymbol1]) // "some-other-id"
console.log(myObject[idSymbol2]) // "some-other-id"
```

Symbol.keyFor() is the opposite of Symbol.for(), and it allows you to retrieve the text value of the symbol key:

```
let someSymbol = Symbol.for("id")
let getSymbolKey = Symbol.keyFor(someSymbol) // "id"
```

Note   In these examples, we set symbols as the keys of our object using square brackets. If you do not use square brackets, JavaScript won't know that you are referring to the variable.

Truthy and Falsy Types

Now that we've covered many of the core principles of types in JavaScript, let's begin looking at how JavaScript handles data which it deems to be true-like or false-like. Since JavaScript doesn't have strongly defined types, a gray area emerges regarding the definitions for the booleans `true` and `false`. Since it makes sense that some values in JavaScript can be considered "sort of" false, like `null` and `undefined`, it's also true that some values can be considered "sort of" true.

These "sort of true" and "sort of false" values are known as truthy and falsy, respectively. The fact that they are only "sort of" true or false has some major implications for how we write code.

The main way this comes into play is in control statements. Truthy statements are coerced to `true` and falsy ones to `false` when used in any control statement. Therefore, `if(null)` would never fire since the `null` becomes `false`, since it is falsy, but `if("string")` would run, since "string" is truthy. The reason "string" is truthy is because a string is not a falsy statement, so by default, it is "truthy".

All examples of `falsy` data are shown in the following, and everything not listed here is therefore considered to be `truthy` instead:

```
// Falsy values in Javascript
NaN          // NaN is falsy
0            // 0 is falsy
-0           // -0 is falsy
undefined    // undefined is falsy
null         // null is falsy
```

```
""           // Empty strings are falsy
' '          // Empty strings are falsy
' '          // Empty strings are falsy
document.all // document.all is the only falsy object
false        // false is of course falsy
```

Truthy and Falsy Operators

Since the concepts of truthy and falsy data have become entrenched in JavaScript, there are some interesting ways to handle them. Some of these will be familiar, but in the context of "truthy/falsy" variables, they will make more sense.

Logical AND Operator

First off, let's look at an operator we discussed when looking at logical statements – the logical AND operator. We used this in earlier chapters to chain conditions for if statements:

```
let x = 5
if(x > 0 && x < 10) {
    console.log("hello world")
}
```

Although usually seen joining logical statements together, it is still, in its simplest form, an operator. While it may seem like all it's doing is acting like the keyword "AND", it's actually doing something else.

What's happening under the hood is the operator is returning the first "falsy" value from either side of && operator and returning that as the value.

In the following example, we're first asking, is x > 0 falsy? If it is, then return its result. Otherwise, it's truthy, so check the next statement. If the next statement is falsy, return it. Otherwise, return the last statement anyway. So the preceding statement actually returns x < 10, which is true, and thus the if statement is true:

```
if(x > 0 && x < 10) {
```

If one of our conditions were false, then the if statement would immediately return it. For example, the following if statement returns the first falsy statement (x < 0), which is false, and thus the if statement never fires. Therefore both sides of the statement must be true for the if statement to fire:

```
let x = 5
if(x < 0 && x < 10) {
    console.log("hello world")
}
```

This means that the logical AND operator can be used in variables too. For example, the following variable myVariable returns "hello world" since x > 0 is truthy:

```
let myVariable = x > 0 && "hello world"
```

Logical OR Operator

We've also encountered the logical OR operator before. In actuality, the OR operator is just the opposite of the logical AND operator. While AND returns the first falsy value, OR returns the first truthy value instead!

Much like AND, then, it can be used in logical statements and variables. The difference is that OR will check if the first value is truthy and return it if it is. Otherwise, if it's falsy, it will return the next value instead:

```
let someValue = 5
let x = 0 || "hello world" // "hello world", since 0 is falsy
let y = null || someValue < 0 // false, since null is falsy, it
returns the second value
let z = "hello world" || 0 // "hello world", since "hello
world" is truthy
```

Nullish Coalescing

What we're seeing here is that falsy and truthy are a little messy. Since data is being coerced into either false or true, some unexpected behavior can occur. For example, falsy can mean all sorts of things, such as 0, undefined, null, document.all, and NaN.

Long after truthy and falsy established themselves in the language, JavaScript came up with the idea of nullish coalescing. This is an alternative to the truthy and falsy behavior seen in logical AND/logical OR operators.

Nullish coalescing, which is indicated by the ?? operator, will only return the second part of a statement if the first is null or undefined. This confines checks to two well-defined primitives, making behavior a little more reliable. In the following code, you can see some examples of how it works in practice:

```
let x = undefined ?? 0 // returns 0
let y = false ?? 0 // returns false
let z = x === 0 ?? 1 // returns true, since x does = 0.
let a = '' ?? true // returns true, since '' is not null or
undefined (it is falsy)
let b = null ?? 5 // returns 5, since null is null or undefined
```

All of the operators we've looked at here, like the logical AND/OR operators, and nullish coalescing operators can be chained. We've looked at this in previous chapters, but let's look at how it executes in the code. For example, we can chain the && operator like so:

```
let x = true && 0 && false
```

Which will ultimately compile to this, since in 0 && false, 0 is the first falsy result:

```
let x = true && 0
```

And then finally to this:

```
let x = 0
```

In summary, there are three operators that take into consideration truthy, falsy, or null-like data:

1. The Logical AND operator, which will return the first value if it's falsy. Otherwise, it will return the second.

2. The Logical OR operator, which will return the first value if it's truthy. Otherwise, it will return the second.

3. Nullish coalescing, which will return the first value if it is not null or undefined. Otherwise, it will return the second.

Optionality

The final topic we will cover in this chapter is optionality. Optionality is another way we can control types. Specifically, optionality allows us to control what happens if an undefined value appears where we didn't expect it to.

Let's consider an example. Imagine we have an API which sends us data in object form. The object sometimes looks like this:

```
let userObject = {
    "name" : "John",
    "age" : "42",
```

```
    "address" : {
        "flatNumber" : "5",
        "streetName" : "Highway Avenue"
        "zipCode" : "12345"
    }
}
```

But what if the API can also send us data in a slightly different from, like this?

```
let userObject = {
    "name" : "John",
    "age" : "42",
    "address" : {
        "houseNumber" : "5",
        "streetName" : "Highway Avenue"
        "locale" : {
            "state" : "AZ",
            "city" : "Cityopolis"
        }
    }
}
```

In this example, sometimes, the address format is different. Ideally, we'd want to fix the object upstream, so we reliably get it in the right format, but that is not always possible.

Imagine a use case where our code depends on a city being available so that we can tell the viewer where John is from:

```
let cityString = 'John is from ${userObject.address.locale.city}'
```

This will work fine if we get an object with the city in it, but if it's missing, then userObject.address.locale.city will return "undefined." Worse still, if locale is missing (like in the first object), then JavaScript will return an error since it cannot get the property "city" of undefined, as undefined is not an object:

```
Uncaught TypeError: Cannot read properties of undefined
(reading 'city')
```

This error is really common in JavaScript and when working with objects since JavaScript does not have a native way to make objects conform to a certain format. One-way programmers used to get around it was by checking every level of an object, to see if it was undefined or not. This requires quite long if statements:

```
if(userObject && userObject.address && userObject.address.
locale && userObject.address.locale.city) {
    let cityString = 'John is from ${userObject.address.
    locale.city}'
}
```

Using this method, we would only ever create cityString if userObject, address, locale, and city were all defined. This works, but it is messy, and that's where optionality comes in.

Optionality lets us short circuit the statement if it finds a value of null or undefined, without throwing an error. To ensure we do not run into errors, we could try running something like this:

```
if(userObject && userObject.address && userObject.address.
locale && userObject.address.locale.city) {
```

However, with optionality, we can greatly simplify this statement. The above statement, for example, could be written like this:

```
if(userObject?.address?.locale?.city) {
```

While this is a lot simpler, it will still return "undefined" if any property in the chain is missing or undefined. That could mean the user would see the word "undefined", which is not something we want.

To avoid this scenario, we can use nullish coalescing to respond with a default value if undefined is returned. This has an additional benefit, in that it means we can remove the if statement altogether:

```
let cityString = 'John is from ${userObject?.address?.locale?.
city ?? "an unknown city"}'
```

Now cityString will return "John is from [[city]]" if a city exists, and it will return "John is from an unknown city" if it does not. Since we didn't need to use an if statement, a cityString is now always available, and not confined within a block scope, even if the city is undefined. Our final code with the userObject looks like this:

```
let userObject = {
    "name" : "John",
    "age" : "42",
    "address" : {
        "houseNumber" : "5",
        "streetName" : "Highway Avenue"
        "locale" : {
            "state" : "AZ",
            "city" : "Cityopolis"
        }
    }
}

let cityString = 'John is from ${userObject?.address?.locale?.
city ?? "an unknown city"}'
```

In summary, optionality gives us two major advantages:

1. Without optionality, we needed to use a lot of nested
    `if` statements. Now we don't need any if statements
    in many cases, reducing the complexity of our code.

2. A missed undefined object could break an entire
    application. Optionality means it won't break but
    just return undefined.

It also gives us one major disadvantage:

1. Optionality can sometimes be used as a "get out of
    jail free card." Instead of fixing your upstream code
    so that it doesn't return undefined, some engineers
    use optionality to skip all errors. This can make
    debugging a big headache.

As with all tools we've looked at in JavaScript, it's important to use
optionality responsibly. If you have a good reason, such as being unable
to influence an upstream piece of software, then using optionality makes
perfect sense. Using optionality without any control, however, can create
more problems for your codebase further down the road.

Summary

In this chapter, we've covered types. We've looked at primitive types,
objects, and their corresponding wrappers. We've explained how
although primitives do not have their own methods or properties, they all
automatically inherit wrappers, which gives them the illusion of having
methods and properties. We've also deep dived into some important
types that we haven't looked at much up until now, like numbers
and dates. We've described how JavaScript's type complexity leads to

interesting problems like truthy and falsy values, and their corresponding operators. Finally, we look at optionality, and how it can be used to contain errors when you don't know that much about a specific object. Types in JavaScript are easy to get started with, but become more complicated as you get deeper into the detail. Having a good grasp of how they work is a requirement for writing good JavaScript code.

CHAPTER 8

Manipulating and Interacting with HTML

So far, we've only been looking at how we can create code to perform certain calculations in JavaScript. At some point, we're going to want to convert that into actual user output which people can see on their screens. Since JavaScript's main purpose has always been to add interactivity to web pages, there are many ways to achieve this.

In this chapter, we'll be looking at how we can use JavaScript and more specifically the document Web API to create interactivity and actually affect what the user sees on the web page.

Window and Document Objects

To start understanding how JavaScript allows us to change what the user sees in the browser, or add interactivity to certain elements like buttons, let's begin by understanding how two critical objects work. There is only one global object in front end browser JavaScript, which we've alluded to already, and this is the `window` object, which can be accessed from anywhere. There is also another object which relates entirely to the HTML document on the window object. These objects are defined below:

© Jonathon Simpson 2023
J. Simpson, *How JavaScript Works*, https://doi.org/10.1007/978-1-4842-9738-4_8

- window is the global this object for browsers.
  It contains many global methods and also key
  information on the window and user.

- document exists on the window object, so it can be
  accessed via window.document. It contains what is
  known as the DOM or document object model, along
  with many useful methods for manipulating and
  interacting with the document.

These two objects are really important for front end development: The window object holds a lot of useful methods and properties on the user and their current activity, such as the current screen size and scroll position. The document object, on the other hand, gives us methods and properties relating to the HTML document itself. For example, document.URL refers to the URL for the current HTML document.

You can get a feel for what is available on both of these objects by console logging them in either your console or a script you are writing.

Note   Since all window methods are available globally, you can skip window. For example, window.alert() is a function used for creating an alert box that the user can't skip. It can be called as just alert(). That is also why you can access document via just document, rather than window.document.

The Window Object

Let's look at how the window object works. The window object (Figure 8-1) has a lot of interesting information about the window that is currently open. For example, you can find the following information on it:

- `window.innerWidth` and `window.innerHeight`, representing the width and height of the window.

- `window.scrollX` and `window.scrollY`, representing the x and y axis scroll positions.

- `window.screenX` and `window.screenY`, representing the x and y coordinates in pixels of the user's cursor.

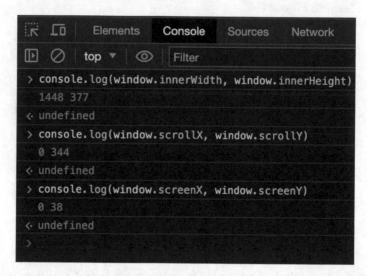

Figure 8-1. *Try console logging some of these window properties. You will find useful values that are used all over the place in web development. These properties are also dynamic:* `window.scrollX` *and* `window.scrollY` *will change as the user scrolls, while* `window. screenX` *and* `window.screenY` *will change as the user moves their cursor*

The `window` object also contains many useful methods and objects, which we have used already. As mentioned, each of these can be accessed without the window prefix:

- `window.console`, which we've used extensively in this book. It is used extensively for logging via `window. console.log`, which is also written as just `console.log`.

- `window.alert()`, which creates an alert box. Although not recommended for general use, it is still used sometimes across the Web. An example of this can be seen in Figure 8-2.

- `window.crypto`, used for creating random UUID values and numbers via `crypto.randomUUID()` and `crypto. getRandomValues()`.

- `window.localStorage()`, for accessing local storage on the browser.

Figure 8-2. *Running a method like `window.alert()` will create an alert box that prevents the page from being interacted with until the user clicks OK*

The Document Object Model

Now that we understand the basics of what the window object contains, let's consider what is contained on the `document`, or `window.document` object. This object contains the **DOM** or document object model, which is a data representation of all HTML tags on your page.

The DOM is an interface that we can interact with via code to change, manipulate, update, and add to the HTML page itself. All HTML, when loaded into a browser, is transformed into a DOM representation. You can see an example of what happens when you console log the DOM in Figure 8-3. Doing this will print out the current HTML page.

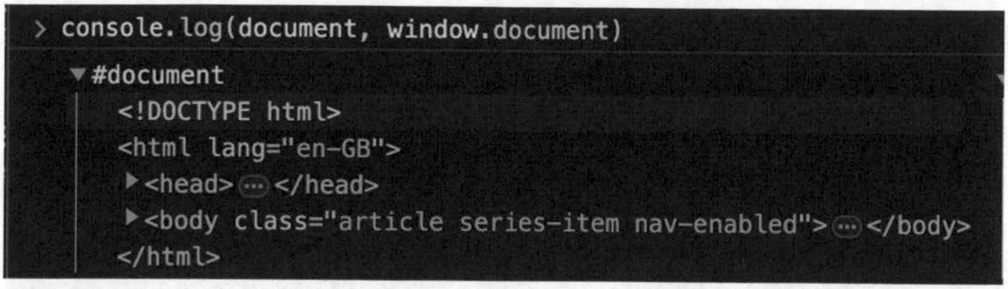

```
> console.log(document, window.document)
  ▼ #document
      <!DOCTYPE html>
      <html lang="en-GB">
      ▶ <head> ⋯ </head>
      ▶ <body class="article series-item nav-enabled"> ⋯ </body>
      </html>
```

Figure 8-3. *Console logging* document *or* window.document *on any web page will return the same thing since they both refer to the same object. In both cases, you'll find a representation of the HTML document returned*

Selecting HTML Elements

All web pages mainly consist of HTML. The HTML loads first, and then scripts or CSS styles will load later depending on where you put them.

If you're familiar with CSS, you'll know that you need to select which HTML elements you want to apply CSS styles to. For example, consider we have an HTML page which looks like this:

```
<!DOCTYPE HTML>
<html>
    <head>
        <title>Hello World Page</title>
    </head>
    <body>
        <p>Hello World</p>
    </body>
</html>
```

In CSS, if we wanted to make the paragraph have red text, it's relatively straightforward to apply a style which does that:

```
p {
    color: red;
}
```

When adding interactivity to web pages, we have the same requirements for element selection, and as such, JavaScript has the same functionality as CSS. For example, what if we wanted the paragraph to do something when the user clicks on it? Or, what if we wanted the paragraph to be red, given some kind of condition?

The four main methods for selection of the DOM via JavaScript are all attached to the document object. After selecting an HTML DOM tag, we can then decide what we want to do with it. The five methods for element selection are as follows:

- `document.querySelectorAll()` – Which will return a list of HTML elements matching a certain criteria

- `document.querySelector()` – Which will return the first matching HTML element found

- `document.getElementById()` – Which will return the first element with a given ID (remember: an HTML ID should be unique, anyway)

- `document.getElementByClassName()` – Which will return a list of HTML elements matching the class you specify

- `document.getElementByTagName()` – Which will return a list of HTML elements matching the tag name you specify, that is, "div"

The Order of HTML

These methods for HTML element selection are dependent on the DOM already having loaded. To illustrate what this means, consider the following example:

```html
<!DOCTYPE HTML>
<html>
    <head>
        <title>Hello World Page</title>
    </head>
    <body>
        <p>Hello World</p>
        <p>Goodbye World</p>
    </body>
    <script type="text/javascript">
        // Our JavaScript
    </script>
</html>
```

Since HTML loads from top to bottom, the location of our JavaScript actually matters. If we put JavaScript at the end of our HTML document, as we have done here, then the DOM will have already loaded by the time the script runs. If the DOM is loaded, we can use methods like document. querySelector() without any concerns.

If you put your JavaScript in the head of the HTML document instead, however, the DOM will not have loaded yet. That means trying to select HTML elements will not work.

In these scenarios, you need to tell JavaScript to wait for the DOM to load. To do that, we need to add what is known as an "event listener," which listens for specific events, to the HTML DOM (or document object) itself. This event listener will "fire" whenever the DOM is loaded, meaning you can only use methods like document.querySelector() within the event listener body:

```
<head>
    <script type="text/javascript">
    document.addEventListener("DOMContentLoaded", (e) => {
        // JavaScript goes here...
    })
    </script>
</head>
```

Sometimes, you won't have a choice on where your JavaScript goes, but if you do, putting your JavaScript at the end of your HTML document is usually easier. Not only can you skip the event listener function, but it means your JavaScript will load last, allowing all your other content to load first. That means faster load times for your user, who can access your page before your JavaScript has been fetched.

With JavaScript at the bottom of our page, we can start selecting elements immediately. In the following example, we use `document.querySelectorAll()` to get a list of all paragraphs:

```
<!DOCTYPE HTML>
<html>
    <head>
        <title>Hello World Page</title>
    </head>
    <body>
        <p class="hello-paragraph">Hello World</p>
        <p id="goodbye">Goodbye World</p>
    </body>
    <script type="text/javascript">
        let allParagraphs = document.querySelectorAll("p")
    </script>
</html>
```

In this example, `allParagraphs` will contain a list of HTML elements that match the selector "p" – which on this page, will be two elements. While you might assume this variable is an array, it is actually a special type of data known as a `NodeList`.

NodeLists and HTMLCollections

`NodeLists`, and their close cousin `HTMLCollections`, are slightly different from arrays. When we use element selector methods, they either generate a `NodeList` or `HTMLCollection`, depending on which one is used:

- `document.querySelectorAll()` returns a `NodeList` of elements. These elements are of type `HTMLElement`.

- `document.querySelector()` returns a single element of type `HTMLElement`.

- `document.getElementById()` returns a single element of type `HTMLElement`.

- `document.getElementByClassName()` returns an `HTMLCollection` of `HTMLElements`.

- `document.getElementByTagName()` returns an `HTMLCollection` of `HTMLElements`.

In simple terms, these are sort of like arrays, but since they do not inherit `Array.prototype`, they lack all of the standard methods that arrays have. They instead inherit from `NodeList.prototype` and `HTMLCollection.prototype`. As usual, console logging either of these will tell you all of the methods available for each as is shown in Figure 8-4.

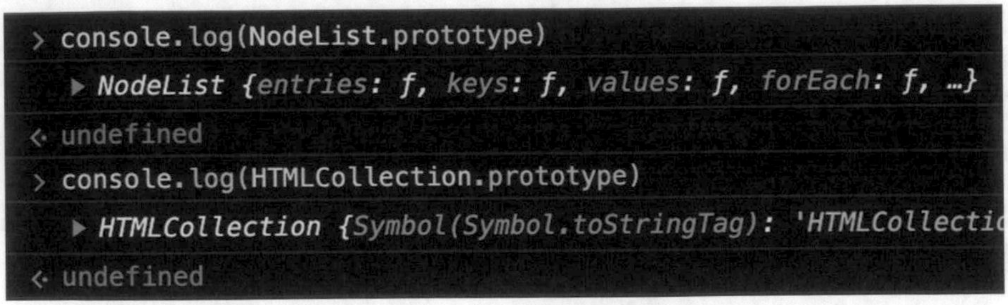

```
> console.log(NodeList.prototype)
  ▸ NodeList {entries: f, keys: f, values: f, forEach: f, …}
⟨∙ undefined
> console.log(HTMLCollection.prototype)
  ▸ HTMLCollection {Symbol(Symbol.toStringTag): 'HTMLCollectic
⟨∙ undefined
```

Figure 8-4. Both NodeLists and HTMLCollections have different prototypes. As such, the methods available on both will be different

There are two major differences between NodeLists and HTMLCollections.

- Firstly, a NodeList contains methods like forEach(), entries(), values(), and keys(), much like objects and arrays do – while HTMLCollections do not.

- Secondly, HTMLCollections are live collections that will update if the HTML DOM updates. NodeLists are static and taken from a certain point in time, so they do not necessarily contain the most up to date information on what is on the page.

In older browsers, both NodeLists and HTMLCollections are neither iterable nor contain the method forEach. Even to this day, HTMLCollections do not have a forEach method.

Due to the limitations of these types, it's common to find both being converted to arrays instead. This allows elements in each to inherit all the useful methods found in Array.prototype. The most common way to convert NodeLists or HTMLCollections to an array is shown in the following example:

```
let allParagraphs = document.querySelectorAll("p")
let nodesToArray = Array.prototype.slice.call(allParagraphs)
```

In the preceding example, we take the slice method straight from Array.prototype and set its context or "this" value to that of the NodeList we wish to convert.

To explain why this works, inside the underlying code for the slice method, this is used to create a shallow copy of an Array. Since a NodeList is a numbered list of elements with a length property, it is close enough to an array to be converted into one. Therefore this code is a backwards compatible way to turn both NodeLists and HTMLCollections into arrays, including in older browsers.

Another way to achieve the same goal is by using the Array.from method instead:

```
let allParagraphs = document.querySelectorAll("p")
let nodesToArray = Array.from(allParagraphs)
```

Either way means we can then iterate over our Array using any array methods, like forEach, or by using a for method like for...of:

```
let allParagraphs = document.querySelectorAll("p")
let nodesToArray = Array.prototype.slice.call(allParagraphs)
nodesToArray.forEach((item) => {
    // Do something with each element...
})
```

Note   You may have heard of libraries and frameworks like jQuery, Angular, React, and Vue. These are libraries that make it easier to create and interact with web pages via JavaScript. All of these libraries build off the fundamentals we are covering here.

Manipulating HTML After Selection

Now that we know how to select HTML elements, let's look at how we can change them. Since a selector like querySelectorAll returns a NodeList, we need to iterate through each item to make sure we apply code to all relevant DOM elements. We can easily do this with a for loop. If you are concerned about old browser support (i.e. pre Chrome 51, Internet Explorer), you can also convert allParagraphs to an array instead, as we showed previously. Otherwise, the code looks like this:

```
let allParagraphs = document.querySelectorAll("p")
for(let item of allParagraphs) {
    item.style.color = "red"
}
```

Here, we used a property available on all HTML elements called style to change the CSS property "color" of each paragraph. An example of how this could look is shown in Figure 8-5. Since querySelectorAll has a forEach method, we could have achieved the same results using that method instead. The code for that is shown in the following example:

```
let allParagraphs = document.querySelectorAll("p")
allParagraphs.forEach((item) => {
    item.style.color = "red"
})
```

Note   forEach loops are typically slower than for loops. If you can use for loop, it's always recommended.

If you only wanted to affect the first paragraph on a page, then you can use querySelector("p"). In this case, you don't need to loop through each item, as only one will be returned.

```
let oneParagraph = document.querySelector("p")
oneParagraph.style.color = "red"
```

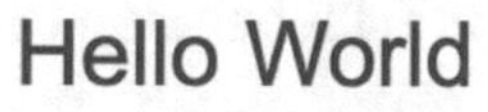

Hello World

Figure 8-5. *Using* `item.style.color` *allows us to programmatically update the text color of HTML elements, as is shown in the preceding image*

When processing a single DOM element in JavaScript, it always inherits methods from `HTMLElement.prototype`. You can find out about all of the methods available to individual HTML DOM elements by using `console.log`:

```
console.log(HTMLElement.prototype)
```

All HTML DOM elements also inherit from another wrapper object called `Element.prototype`. The additional methods inherited from `Element.prototype` can also be console logged. You can see the output for both of these prototypes in Figure 8-6.

```
console.log(Element.prototype)
```

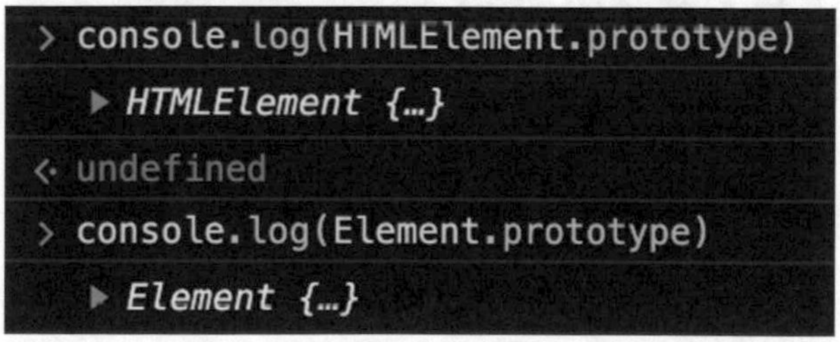

Figure 8-6. *You can find all methods on* `HTMLElements` *by console logging the preceding two prototypes. Events can also be found. For example,* `HTMLElements` *have the method* `onclick`*, which represents the "click" event*

171

So far we've only looked at generic queries to select HTML elements using methods like querySelectorAll, but we can also select elements based on their specific ID using getElementById too. This will return only one element since IDs in HTML should be unique. If your HTML document contains more than one tag with the same ID by accident, then getElementById will only return the first element. This method is slightly faster, so it's preferable where possible to use.

In the following example, we style all paragraphs to have the text color red, and then we style any with the ID "goodbye" in green.

Since goodbyeParagraph is still a paragraph, the first part of our code will set its color to red initially. Then, when we apply the color green to it, it will overwrite red – resulting in one red paragraph and another in green. You can see the outcome of this in Figure 8-7.

HTML:

```
<p class="hello-paragraph">Hello World</p>
<p id="goodbye">Goodbye World</p>
```

JavaScript:

```
let allParagraphs = document.querySelectorAll("p")
let goodbyeParagraph = document.getElementById("goodbye")
for(let item of allParagraphs) {
    item.style.color = "red"
}

goodbyeParagraph.style.color = "green"
```

Hello World

Goodbye World

Figure 8-7. *How our HTML page looks after applying CSS styles via JavaScript to* allParagraphs *and* goodbyeParagraph

Adding Events to HTML Elements

Now that we understand that you can select HTML elements using a variety of document methods, let's look at how we can add user interactivity to specific HTML elements.

To do that, we use a standard method found on all HTMLElements called addEventListener. This method accepts three arguments. The first is the type of event which the user is performing, like click, hover, etc, and the second is a function that fires when the event is triggered (i.e., what happens if a user clicks a button). The third argument is an optional object containing additional options which are applied to the event.

Let's look at an example to better illustrate this. Consider a user case wherewe want to add an event to a <div> with ID "click-me" whenever the user clicks that <div>. First we select the element using getElementById(). Then we add the event listener. In this case, the event is called "click." In the following code, whenever someone clicks an element with ID "click-me," a console will fire saying, "Hello World!".

```
let getDiv = document.getElementById("click-me")
getDiv.addEventListener("click", function(e) {
    console.log("Hello World!")
});
```

Creating a Modal Window

The previous example is relatively straightforward to understand, but not very useful in real life. A more common functionality created using event listeners are modal popup windows which appear when the user clicks a button on a website. Let's look at how we can create one of these modal window using the concepts we've already looked at so far. First, let's create a basic HTML page as is shown in the following example:

```
<!DOCTYPE HTML>
<html>
    <head>
        <title>Hello World Page</title>
        <style>
            #main-text {
                opacity: 0;
            }
        </style>
    </head>
    <body>
        <button id="click-me">Click Me</button>
        <p id="main-text">Main Text</p>
    </body>
</html>
```

While this page has no interactivity by default, we can change that with JavaScript. You'll notice that in our CSS, #main-text is hidden by setting its opacity to 0. Let's write some JavaScript so that if the user clicks the button, "#main-text" will have it's opacity adjusted to 1, so that it appears:

```
let getButton = document.getElementById("click-me")
getButton.addEventListener("click", function(e) {
    let getMainText = document.getElementById("main-text")
    getMainText.style.opacity = 1
});
```

Using this code, whenever a user clicks a button with the ID "click-me," we fire off a function that sets the opacity of "main-text" to 1. This has one problem, though: it only works once! When the user clicks the button, it can only set the opacity of "Main Text" to 1. What if we want it to appear or hide every time the button is clicked?

To do that, we can use CSS classes, and luckily all HTMLElements have methods to alter CSS classes. These methods are found on HTMLElement. classList. Let's first change the HTML layout so that we have a separate class for hidden elements with opacity values of 0. With a setup like this, we don't need to rely on adding styles directly to the element #main-text anymore. Instead, we can change the class which the HTML element has:

```
<!DOCTYPE HTML>
<html>
    <head>
        <title>Hello World Page</title>
        <style>
            .hidden {
                opacity: 0;
            }
        </style>
    </head>
    <body>
        <button id="click-me">Click Me</button>
        <p id="main-text" class="hidden">Main Text</p>
    </body>
</html>
```

In this HTML, #main-text is hidden by a CSS class called .hidden. In JavaScript, we can change if #main-text has this class but using the toggle method classList.toggle("hidden"). When run, this method will check if #main-text has the CSS class hidden. If it does, it will remove it; otherwise, it will add it:

```
let getButton = document.getElementById("click-me")
getButton.addEventListener("click", function(e) {
    let getMainText = document.getElementById("main-text")
    getMainText.classList.toggle("hidden")
});
```

Using this simple code, we've immediately added interactivity to our web page. Worth noting is the fact that classList contains other useful methods:

- `HTMLElement.classList.contains("class")` – For checking if an HTML element contains a certain class

- `HTMLElement.classList.add("class")` – For adding a class to an element

- `HTMLElement.classList.remove("class")` – For removing a class from an element

- `HTMLElement.classList.replace("oldClass", "newClass")` – For replacing a class with a new class

Creating a Counter

To further our understanding of how we can interact with the HTML DOM, let's look at another example. In this simple example we will create a counter which increases every time the user clicks a button. Let's start by creating an HTML page that contains both our counter and a button to increase it:

```
<div id="counter">0</div>
<button id="plus-button">
  Click Me
</button>
```

Next let's create the JavaScript we'll need to make this work. In the following example, we check for click events on the "plus-button" element. When one occurs, we take the text value from "counter" and parse it into a number using a method we've covered before, called parseInt. We add 1 to that number and then show that new number to the user by inserting it into the counter element. This is illustrated in the following code, and you can also seehow this looks in Figure 8-8.

```
let button = document.getElementById("plus-button")

button.addEventListener("click", function(e) {
      let counter = document.getElementById("counter")
  let counterValue = parseFloat(counter.textContent)
  counter.textContent = counterValue + 1
})
```

Figure 8-8. *Using everything we've learned so far, we can create a simple counter like the one shown earlier*

Event Types

In the previous examples, we've only looked at the click event, but there are loads of other useful events in JavaScript too. The following is a list of the events most important to HTMLElements, and the ones you'll find yourself using the most.

Event Name	Description
click	When a user clicks the page with a mouse.
scroll	When a user scrolls inside an HTML element. Can also be applied to the document in general.
dblclick	When a user double-clicks.
keydown, keypress, keyup	When a user presses a key down (keydown), when it has been pressed (keypress), and then when it has been released (keyup).
mouseup, mousedown, mousemove	When a user clicks down (mousedown), releases their mouse button (mouseup), and moves their mouse while it is pressed down (mousemove).
mouseleave, mouseout	For handling when a user moves their mouse out of an element. mouseout will only fire once, while mouseleave will fire for every div it leaves.
touchstart, touchend, touchmove	When a user touches on a touch device (touchstart), and when they lift their finger (touchend). When a user moves their finger, many touchmove events will fire.
pointerdown, pointerup, pointermove	This replicates touchdown/mousedown, touchup/mouseup, and touchmove/mousemove combined.
pointerout, pointerleave, pointerenter	pointerout and pointerleave replicates mouseout/mouseleave. pointerenter is when the user's pointer enters a specific element.

Note   While we're covering vents pertinent to HTML elements in this chapter, it's worth noting that other types of data may have event listeners too. As we saw earlier, the document object itself has specific events like DOMContentLoaded.

Pointers, Touch, and Mouse

The events click, scroll, resize, and dblclick are relatively self-explanatory. A common question that tends to crop up is the question of why we seem to have duplicates for mousedown, mousemove, and mouseup. For example:

- For "up" events, we have mouseup/pointerup/touchup.

- For "down" events, we have mousedown/pointerdown/touchdown.

- For move events, we have mousemove/pointermove/touchmove.

As with most anomalies in JavaScript, the reason is historical. When JavaScript started, there weren't really any touch devices – and even when touch devices were becoming popular, JavaScript was slow to react. So in the beginning, JavaScript only saw the need for three events:

- mousedown – For when the user pressed their mouse button down

- mousemove – For when they moved it

- mouseup – For when they released it

This allowed us to do some neat things which click could not achieve. For example, we could store information on when the user pressed their mouse down and then do something if they continued to move it. In the following example, we can test if the mouse is down by using the mouseup and mousedown event listeners and a variable that stores that state. Then we can check on this variable to do something specific if the user moves their mouse while it is clicked:

```
let isMouseDown = false
document.addEventListener("mousedown", function(e) {
    isMouseDown = true
```

```
})
document.addEventListener("mousemove", function(e) {
    if(isMouseDown) {
        console.log("The user is dragging!")
    }
})
document.addEventListener("mouseup", function(e) {
    isMouseDown = true
})
```

This kind of setup was most frequently seen when trying to add drag and drop to web pages. When touch devices came, it complicated things. We couldn't really remove mouse events, but we needed new ones for touch. So JavaScript added touch equivalents: touchdown, touchmove, and touchup.

As device user experience began to merge across both mouse based devices and touch devices, and code bases became more and more complicated, having these two separate events became a bit of a nuisance. To remedy this final problem, JavaScript created three new events: pointerdown, pointermove and pointerup. These fire for both touch and mouse events, meaning there is no need to run both events separately.

The reason we have three is historical, but it is also sometimes useful. For example, we can detect if someone is interacting via a touch device, just by checking for the touchdown event firing:

```
document.addEventListener("touchdown", function(e) {
    // Touch device
})
```

Event Capturing, Targeting, and Bubbling

Let's deep dive into how events actually work under the surface. When an event fires, they follow four main steps, and they make intuitive sense. How this works can also be seen in Figure 8-9.

1. First, the user performs an event. For example, they click an element.

2. Then, the event is applied to the element, known as **the target phase**.

3. Most events bubble up from where the event occurs. For example, a click may occur deep in the DOM, but this will trigger an event listener on all parent elements too, known as **the bubble phase.**

4. An alternative way of triggering events can also occur. This is where events propagate from the top down. If this is used, it is known as **the capture phase**.

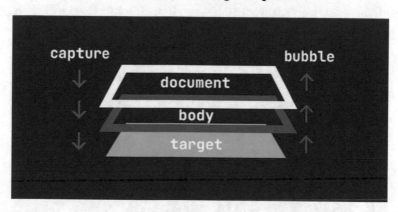

Figure 8-9. *When an event is performed by the user, JavaScript can either propagate the event from the top down or the bottom up*

By default, all events fire by bubbling. To understand the concept of bubbling, consider the following HTML:

```html
<div id="my-div">
    <div class="some-div">
        <p class="paragraph">Hello World</p>
    </div>
</div>
```

If we have some JavaScript adding an event to #my-div, something interesting happens:

```
document.getElementById("my-div").addEventListener("click"...
```

If the user performs an event (e.g., click) on .paragraph, we also have to remember that it is contained within #my-div. While the user clicked .paragraph, they are technically also clicking #my-div. So the event you performed bubbles up from where the event happened to #my-div, firing the addEventListener we had for #my-div.

In other words, the event the user applied to an element bubbles up through the DOM. Similarly, if #my-div is within the body tag, then a click event assigned to the body will still fire if #my-div is clicked. As such, the event bubbles up from where it happened, until it hits the item with an event listener. This is illustrated in Figure 8-10.

Figure 8-10. Some events will bubble up to the next element in the DOM by default. Clicking #my-div also counts as a click on body and document

Bubbling can be prevented in an event by running e.stopPropagation within it. This function exists on the e variable that comes with all events. That will confine a click or event to the element you apply it to:

```
document.addEventListener("click", function(e) {
    e.stopPropagation()
})
```

There is also a method called e.stopImmediatePropagation, which has a similar name but is slightly different. Not only will e.stopImmediatePropagation stop further bubbling of an event upward, but it will also stop any further event handlers of that type from being added to the element. For example, if you used e.stopImmediatePropagation within a click event for an element, any other click events added to that element would not work.

Note: Some events do not bubble, and these are listed below:

- scroll – Since you only ever scroll in one element, and a scroll should not cause another scroll somewhere else.

- load – Since you tend to apply this event to check if certain elements have loaded – for example, document. addEventListener("load"), to check if the DOM has loaded.

- focus – Since you focus on only one element. This event is fired, for example, if you focus in on a form element.

- blur – The opposite of focus, so the same applies as for focus.

Capturing Phase

We can force events to fire via capturing instead of bubbling. This ultimately has the impact of changing the order in which events occur. Consider again our example from earlier:

```
<div id="my-div">
    <div class="some-div">
        <p class="paragraph">Hello World</p>
    </div>
</div>
```

In this example, we had some JavaScript tying an event to #my-div:

```
document.getElementById("my-div").addEventListener("click",
someEvent)
```

If we click .paragraph, this is what happens by default:

- The click event is performed by the user.

- The event is then applied to the target itself, which in this case, was .paragraph.

- The event moves into the **bubbling** phase, and someEvent is executed.

To change this to capture, addEventListener has a third argument though, where we can store options. Using this, we can configure an event to fire during capture:

```
document.getElementById("my-div").addEventListener("click",
someEvent, { capture: true })
```

Using this code, the same thing happens from a user perspective, but it's subtly different in terms of code execution:

- The click event is performed by the user.

- JavaScript starts from the top down. For example, the browser would apply click events to html → body → #my-div.

- In bubbling, the order would have been .paragraph →
  .some-div → #my-div. JavaScript goes down the DOM
  to find the element.

Setting an event to capture is not really used a lot, but it can come in useful in some scenarios, where we want events to fire slightly earlier than they otherwise would, since events applied in the capture phase always happen before those applied via bubbling.

Other Event Options

As we just mentioned, addEventListener has a third option where we can apply additional configuration:

```
el.addEventListener("click", (e) => {

}, {
    capture: true,
    once: false,
    passive: true
})
```

Along with capture, which we have already covered, there are two other options:

- once, which if set to true will cause an event to only fire
  on the first attempt. By default, it is set to false.

- passive, which prevents the behavior of
  e.preventDefault(). By default, it is set to false –
  except for wheel, mousewheel, touchstart, and
  touchmove on non-Safari browsers, where it is set
  to true.

The first two options are straightforward given what we've discussed already, but the last requires some explanation.

First of all, e.preventDefault() is another method found on the e variable. It prevents the default behavior that an event would cause upon an HTML element, for example, e.preventDefault() applied to click events on check boxes, preventing those check boxes from being checked. Similarly, when applied to links, it stops those links from being clicked. In the following code, for example, we use this function to prevent all links on a page from being clicked:

```
let anchors = document.querySelectorAll('a')

for(let x of anchors) {
    x.addEventListener('click', (e) => {
        e.preventDefault()
    })
}
```

Another use can be disabling certain keys. You could do this by using e.code, which contains the key clicked for keyboard events:

```
document.getElementById("form-input").
addEventListener("keydown", function(e) {
    if(e.code = "KeyE") {
        console.log("Don't press the e key!")
        e.preventDefault()
    }
})
```

This works since JavaScript events come before the actual default behavior of inputs. That means your code fires before the actual key is shown on the screen.

Now, let's go back to the passive option. The main use case for setting passive to true on an event is to improve scrolling for wheel, touchmove, touchstart, and mousewheel events. Beyond this, it does not have much utility. Most browsers even do this by default now, but Safari does not. As such, you will need to enable passive for these events to ensure they work smoothly in Safari.

The reason this improves scrolling is because all browsers have features built in to ensure smooth scrolling. Events like wheel, which also causes scrolling, interfere with this and thus have much reduced performance when compared to scroll. By promising JavaScript that we won't prevent default scrolling behavior on these events, JavaScript is freed up to process the scrolling immediately – resulting in much smoother scrolling.

Live Data Using Events

Earlier in this chapter we discussed how the window object contains many useful properties such as the mouse position and window size. While useful, this data is not live. If you try to console log it, you'll only get its value for a point in time:

```
console.log(window.innerWidth) // The window width, at this
point in time
```

To get live data, we need to couple these properties with event listeners. Let's consider an example where we add a class to a header element when the screen width is below 700 pixels.

First, it's important to know that the window object also has some important event listeners, like resize and scroll. The resize event will fire for every pixel change in the window size, meaning we can track the live window size using this event listener:

```
window.addEventListener("resize", function(e) {
    let getHeader = document.getElementById("top-banner")
    console.log(`The screen width is ${window.innerWidth}px`)
    if(window.innerWidth < 700) {
        getHeader.classList.add("small")
    }
})
```

This can be used more simply to gain live data on screen or window size, as is shown in the following example. You can see the result of this code in Figure 8-11.

```
let screenWidth = window.innerWidth
window.addEventListener("resize", function(e) {
    screenWidth = window.innerWidth
    console.log(`The screen width is ${screenWidth}px`)
})
```

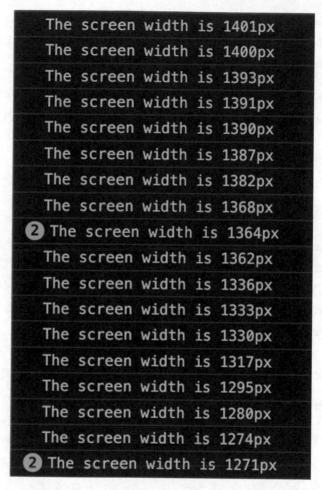

Figure 8-11. *Applying an event like resize to a window will cause it to fire many times if the user is resizing. This gives us flexibility to understand the current width of the window the user is using*

We can use the same concept to capture live data on the user's mouse position. This is really important in use cases like drag-and-drop. If we want to know the live position of the user's mouse cursor or finger in a touch setting, we have to use an event since the window and document properties only hold information on what the state was when the page

189

loaded. Code like that in the following will contain live information on a user's finger or mouse position as they move it. Any movement will result in a new console line, just like any resize did in Figure 8-11.

```
document.body.addEventListener("pointermove", function(e) {
    console.log(`The user's position is X: ${e.pageX}px Y: ${e.
pageY}px`)
})
```

Drag and Drop

To help us summarize everything we've learned so far. and a few other new concepts, let's create a drag-and-drop demo. In this demo, we'll create a square div which we'll be able to drag across the screen and drop somewhere else. Then, if we try to drag it again, we'll be able to drag it somewhere else.

For this to work, we're going to need some HTML and CSS. For our HTML, we'll only create the div which we'll soon be able to drag:

```
<div id="drag"></div>
```

For our CSS, we'll make a simple red square div:

```
#drag {
    background: red;
    width: 70px;
    height: 70px;
    position: relative;
    margin: 20px;
    left: 0;
    top: 0;
    color: white;
}
```

Note   We'll be using relative positioning to move the div. As such, it's important we set a default left and top value so that we don't create a NaN value in our code.

We will utilize two new functions we haven't seen before to make this work. These two functions, getComputedStyle and getPropertyValue, will let us retrieve the current CSS properties for a given HTML element.

Let's start by creating the bare bones we'll need to add dragging to the div we've created earlier. The comments in the following example should also help you understand what is going on:

```
// Select the div we want to drag
let drag = document.getElementById("drag")
// getComputedStyle gets all CSS for an element
let dragCss = getComputedStyle(drag)

let dragging = false // Set to true if dragging is happening

// These two variables store information
let initialMousePosition = [ 0, 0 ]
let initialBlockPosition = [ 0, 0 ]

drag.addEventListener("mousedown", (e) => {
    dragging = true
    initialMousePosition = [ e.screenX, e.screenY ]
    initialBlockPosition = [
        dragCss.getPropertyValue("left"),
        dragCss.getPropertyValue("top")
    ]
})

drag.addEventListener("mouseup", (e) => {
    dragging = false
})
```

Let's break down what is happening here in more detail

- First, we select the div element #drag and store it in a variable called drag. We then create another variable for getting all CSS properties associated with drag, called dragCss.

- Then we create three variables for storing information on the drag. The variable dragging is set to true if mousedown fires and false if mouseup fires instead. When mousedown fires, we also store the initial mouse position in initialMousePosition.

- Finally, we also retrieve the initial CSS properties for "left" and "top" in initialBlockPosition using the getPropertValue() function.

Note   If you're not familiar with CSS, the left and top properties allow you to move an element by a certain amount from its original location. Both left and top push the element from the left and top by a certain amount, respectively.

Now let's add the actual drag event. For this to work, we need to calculate how much the user has moved their mouse by subtracting their initial mouse position from wherever they've moved to. We will only do this if the dragging variable is true, which implies the user has clicked their mouse down on the draggable div.

All we need to do now is add this modification value to the left and top values in initialBlockPosition and set the <div>'s CSS to match the new value. We can then apply this number as a CSS left and top value to move the div. I've also updated the element's innerHTML so that it contains information on the <div>'s current coordinates. The code for this is shown in the following example, and can also be seen in Figure 8-12.

```
document.addEventListener("mousemove", (e) => {
    if(dragging) {
        let x = parseFloat(initialBlockPosition[0])
        let y = parseFloat(initialBlockPosition[1])

        let modificationX = e.screenX - initialMousePosition[0]
        let modificationY = e.screenY - initialMousePosition[1]

        drag.style.left = `${x + modificationX}px`
        drag.style.top = `${y + modificationY}px`

        drag.innerHTML = `x: ${x + modificationX}pxSPi-Amp-
LessThanbr /SPi-Amp-GreaterThan y: ${y + modificationY}px`
    }
})
```

Figure 8-12. *Using the tools we've learned about so far, we can add drag-and-drop functionality to our web pages by calculating the position of a* <div> *element*

The e variable

We've touched on a lot of important concepts around event listening and DOM manipulation. In these examples, we've used methods from a variable called e, which is available to all events when we called our event listener function:

```
getButton.addEventListener("click", function(e) {
```

If you console log e, it contains a lot of information about the event which is currently firing. It tends to contain information relevant to the event – for example, if your event was a click event, it will tell you the pageX and pageY – which is the x and y coordinates of where the user clicked.

This can be used to your advantage – for example, if you wanted something to happen when the user clicked somewhere on your document, but only beyond an x position of 500 pixels and a y position of 200 pixels. This might be useful if you want to record click events in a certain part of the screen, but not in another, like what happens in a web application with an interactable area:

```
document.body.addEventListener("click", function(e) {
    if(e.pageX > 500 && e.pageY > 200) {
        console.log("Hello World!")
    }
})
```

As we saw earlier, the e variable also contains information on the key pressed via e.code on key press events:

```
document.getElementById("form-input").
addEventListener("keydown", function(e) {
    console.log(`You pressed a key with the key code ${e.code}`)
})
```

Since e is just a variable, you can console log it too. You can see an example of the e variable for a click event in Figure 8-13.

```
▼ PointerEvent {isTrusted: true, pointerId: 1, width: 1, height: 1,
    isTrusted: true
    altKey: false
    altitudeAngle: 1.5707963267948966
    azimuthAngle: 0
    bubbles: true
    button: 0
    buttons: 0
    cancelBubble: false
    cancelable: true
    clientX: 495
    clientY: 143
    composed: true
    ctrlKey: false
    currentTarget: null
    defaultPrevented: false
    detail: 1
    eventPhase: 0
    fromElement: null
    height: 1
    isPrimary: false
    layerX: 445
```

Figure 8-13. *The e variable is invaluable for events and can tell you all sorts of useful information about what the user did in the event. Here is an example for a click event*

Creating New Elements with JavaScript

We've now covered how we select elements and how we add events to them, and how those events work – but what if we want to create new HTML? For example, what if instead of just toggling some CSS, we wanted to create a new HTML element from scratch when the user does something? Well that's also possible with JavaScript using another document method called document.createElement:

```
let newEl = document.createElement("div")
```

We can make any element this way. Just change "div" in the following example to the kind of element you want to make. Once we initiate the creation of an element, we need to use some other methods and properties to define how that element should be. In the following example, along with using style and classList, we also use setAttribute to create a custom attribute for newEl:

```
let newEl = document.createElement("div")

newEl.style.color = "red"
// Let's add a class called 'active' to it
newEl.classList.add("active")
// Let's add an attribute called 'data-attribute'
newEl.setAttribute("data-attribute", true)
```

To change what appears as text content inside of this element, we can use the property, textContent:

```
// Let's add some text inside the div
newEl.textContent = "I am a created element."
```

If we want to add HTML instead, we can use innerHTML to set the HTML inside this new element:

```
// Let's add some text inside the div
newEl.innerHTML = "<p>Hello World</p>"
```

Note   Use innerHTML with care. While it is OK to use this in local applications in many cases, it can be used maliciously by hackers to add HTML you didn't want. Always check the content going into innerHTML and make sure you trust it!

While this has allowed us to make an HTML element, it still only exists in JavaScript! So how do we actually add it to our HTML page? To do that, we need to use a few methods that exist on all HTMLElements.

You can only really insert new HTML in JavaScript in relation to other HTML. The methods and properties we have at our disposal to do that are as follows:

- HTMLElement.prepend() – For adding a new HTML element directly inside the HTMLElement, at the start

- HTMLElement.append() – For adding a new HTML element directly inside the HTMLElement, at the end

- HTMLElement.before() – For adding a new HTML element before a specified element

- HTMLElement.after() – For adding a new HTML element after a specified element

- HTMLElement.innerHTML – For directly changing all the inner HTML of an element into something else

To demonstrate how this works, imagine we have some HTML that looks like this:

```
<div id="my-div">
    <div class="some-div">
        Some Text
    </div>
    <p class="para">Hello World</p>
    <p class="para-2">Hello World</p>
</div>
```

We now also have some JavaScript for creating a new element:

```
let newEl = document.createElement("div")

newEl.style.color = "red"
// Let's add a class called 'active' to it
newEl.classList.add("active")
// Let's add an attribute called 'data-attribute'
newEl.setAttribute("data-attribute", true)
// Let's add some text inside the div
newEl.textContent = "I am a created element."
// Let's give our element an ID
newEl.id = "master-element"
```

We can insert this new element, newEl, into the HTML document via reference to another HTML element. For example, we can prepend newEl to the beginning of #my-div:

```
let findMyDiv = document.getElementById("my-div")
findMyDiv.prepend(newEl)
```

After doing this, if we look at our HTML we will see something like this:

```
<div id="my-div">
    <div id="master-element" data-attribute="true"
style="color: red;" class="active">I am a created element</div>
    <div class="some-div">
        Some Text
    </div>
    <p class="para">Hello World</p>
    <p class="para-2">Hello World</p>
</div>
```

The append method works in the same way, only it adds the element to the end rather than the start of an element. If we want to get more specific about where we insert elements, rather than just adding it within another element at the start or end, we need to use before and after. For example, the following code would insert newEl directly after the .para element:

```
let findThePara = document.querySelector(".para")
newEl.after(findThePara)
```

Manipulating CSS with JavaScript

We've already touched upon how we can change CSS with JavaScript through the style property. Now let's look at these properties in more depth.

HTMLElements and Changing Styles in JavaScript

The style property on HTMLElements allows for the manipulation of all CSS properties. You can see some of these in the following example:

```
myEl.style.position = "relative"
myEl.style.left = "500px"
myEl.style.marginLeft = "10px"
myEl.style.color = "red"
myEl.style.width = "500px"
myEl.style.height = "500px"
myEl.style.padding = "0 0 0 10px"
```

In general, CSS styles are converted to camel case in JavaScript. So while the CSS property for a left margin is called margin-left, in JavaScript it becomes style.marginLeft. These rules are typically consistent, but there is one exception, that being that float is referred to as cssFloat.

Adding New Style Sheets to HTML Pages

While the style property on HTMLElement is by far the most common way to set CSS in JavaScript, it is not the only way. It's also possible to add new CSS rules directly into existing CSS style sheets in your HTML document. All CSS style sheets can be found on the object document.styleSheets as an array. This includes CSS imported via link HTML tags and inline CSS. The imported CSS comes first and then the inline CSS later.

Stylesheets are also their own type of data, with each being known as a CSSStyleSheet. That means, as you might expect by now, they inherit a bunch of useful style sheet methods from CSSStyleSheet.prototype. One of these methods is insertRule, which lets you wholesale add new CSS blocks into existing style sheets. In the following example, we add CSS to the first style sheet found (index 0):

```
// This line gets our first style sheet file
let style = window.document.styleSheets[0]
// Then we insert our rule. In this case, our rule is p {
color: black; }
style.insertRule("p { color: black; }")
```

It's also worth noting that another method called deleteRule() exists, which deletes a certain block of CSS from a style sheet at a certain index. For example, deleteRule(0) would delete the first block of CSS found in a stylesheet.

Setting CSS Variables

It's quite common to create CSS variables in a stylesheet, and therefore it can be useful to change these CSS variables with your code. Since CSS rules usually apply to the root of the document, this is a little tricky. A useful property found on the document object which we can use for this is document.documentElement. This object refers to the root of the document – in other words, the <html> tag, and is similar to how we can select the body of an HTML document using document.body.

Since the HTML tag itself is also an HTML element, we can add CSS variables directly to it using a style method we have not covered before – setProperty. We do it this way by adding the variables to the HTML tag itself so that they are available at the root of the CSS document for any other CSS to use.

Using setProperty on the document element, we can create CSS variables, as is shown in the following example:

```
document.documentElement.style.setProperty('--my-background-color', 'red')
document.documentElement.style.setProperty('--my-text-color', 'white')
```

Getting CSS Properties and HTML Dimensions

In the previous section, we created a drag-and-drop <div> where we got the current left and top CSS properties via the following code:

```
// Select the div we want to drag
let drag = document.getElementById("drag")
// getComputedStyle gets all CSS for an element
let dragCss = getComputedStyle(drag)
left dragLeft = dragCss.getPropertyValue("left")
let dragTop = dragCss.getPropertyValue("top")
```

To get CSS properties, we need to use getPropertValue and getComputedStyle. That's because while the style property on HTMLElements lets us *set* the value of style properties, it does not let us *get* them.

CSS properties like those mentioned earlier ultimately contribute to the final position of an HTML element on the page. The position of an element is also determined by its location inside the HTML document and CSS properties like margin.

To get the specific position of an HTML element in pixels (using the top left corner of the screen as the reference point), we have to use another method that exists on all HTML elements called getBoundingClientRect(). Using this, we can get properties like the x or left position of a div from the left-hand side of the page. This is illustrated in the following example:

```
// Select the div we want to drag
let drag = document.getElementById("drag")
let positionLeft = drag.getBoundingClientRect().left
```

This means we can get the current location of any HTML element on demand. The getBoundingClientRect() function can also be used to get information on the top, left, bottom, right, x, y, width, and height of any HTMLElement. In the following example, we are able to get the width, x position, and bottom position of "drag":

```
// Select the div we want to drag
let drag = document.getElementById("drag")
let positionX = drag.getBoundingClientRect().x
let positionBottom = drag.getBoundingClientRect().bottom
let positionWidth = drag.getBoundingClientRect().width
```

This function comes in useful when building interactive web experiences, where knowing the position of HTML elements can help with things like drag and drop. For example, we might use this to check if a user dropped an element on top of another, so that they could be stacked together. A diagram of which coordinates getBoundingClientRect() uses for each property can be seen in Figure 8-14.

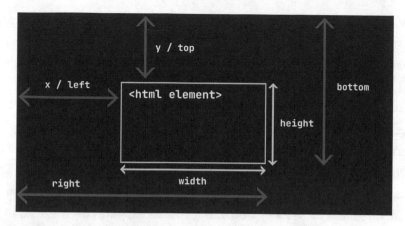

Figure 8-14. *The* getBoundingClientRect *function is another powerful tool for getting information on the current position of any HTML element*

Summary

In this chapter, we've covered how to start working with HTML in JavaScript. We've discussed how to select HTML elements using a variety of different methods and then how to manipulate those elements using some other HTML specific methods. We then covered user events and how to track them so that you can do things when a user interacts with your web page.

We've looked at the different wrapper objects assigned to HTML elements and collections, like HTMLElement, Element, HTMLCollection, and NodeList. We have also discussed how you can find out more about the methods and properties available to you via the console log by using console.log(HTMLElement.prototype). You can also learn more online about these prototypes and methods via websites like *developer. mozilla.org.*

We've also learned how to create HTML elements programmatically via JavaScript- and how to change CSS too. Finally, we've looked at how you can find the location of any HTML element on a page using specific HTML element methods.

This chapter has covered all of the basics which you'll need to get started, but there is so much more to learn beyond this. The best way to learn is by experimentation! Using the examples we've covered in this chapter, why not try building your own interactivity into web pages? Try playing around in your web browser's console, in your own JavaScript files, or via online tools like *jsfiddle.net*. You can expand on these examples quite easily. For instance, you could turn the drag-and-drop example into a fully fledged whiteboard. As you start to explore what's possible, you'll learn more and become even more familiar with the concepts we've covered here.

CHAPTER 9

Maps and Sets

While `objects` and `arrays` are the most common way of storing data in JavaScript, they do have some limitations. For example, neither objects nor arrays have the ability to create a unique list without duplicates. Similarly, objects cannot contain keys that are not `strings` or `symbols`. To overcome these challenges and more, two additional special types of `objects` exist known as **maps** and **sets**. Both of these have unique functionality, which makes them well-suited to certain tasks. In this chapter, we'll be diving into both of these `objects` and when to use them.

Sets

Sets are mutable lists of values, which are quite similar to arrays. The difference between sets and arrays is that sets cannot contain duplicates. This makes them very performant for tasks where you need to have a unique list. If you try to add a duplicate item to a set, it will automatically be rejected without throwing an error.

Creating a set is relatively simple. All you need is the constructor, `Set()`, and then special methods like add and remove to modify it:

```
let mySet = new Set()
mySet.add(4)
mySet.add(4)

console.log(mySet) // Set(1) {4}
```

© Jonathon Simpson 2023
J. Simpson, *How JavaScript Works*, https://doi.org/10.1007/978-1-4842-9738-4_9

Note   If you try to add duplicate values to a set, only one will be added. Sets automatically reject duplicate values.

Sets will only support the addition of unique values for primitives, but with objects, they use an object's reference instead of its value. That means it is possible to add two objects which have the same value but have different references. This is shown in the following example:

```
let mySet = new Set()
mySet.add({ "name" : "John" })
mySet.add({ "name" : "John" })

// Set(2) {{ "name" : "John" }, { "name" : "John" }}
console.log(mySet)
```

Sets also handle equality in a slightly different way than we've looked at so far. Sets will consider NaN to be equal to NaN even though in previous examples we should that NaN === NaN and NaN == NaN returns `false`. The reason why sets work this way is because they use a slightly different equality algorithm. These equality algorithms are summarized below:

- The `IsLooselyEqual` equality algorithm is applied when we use double equals (==) and matches on value.

- The `IsStrictlyEqual` equality algorithm is applied when we use triple equals (===) and matches on value/type.

- The `SameValueZero` is used by sets. It considers both value and type in equality like `IsStrictlyEqual` but also considers NaN to be equal to NaN.

As such, if we try to add two NaNs to a set, the result is that only one gets added:

```
let mySet = new Set()
mySet.add(NaN)
mySet.add(NaN)

// Set(1) {NaN}
console.log(mySet)
```

Note   Sets are really useful when you have an array where duplicates are not allowed. It's always possible for faulty code to let duplicates into an array which should not have any, but sets ensure that this will never happen.

Modifying Sets

Sets are mutable like other objects, and we mutate them via special set methods. The three main methods for changing a set are:

- Set.add() – To add an item to your set
- Set.delete() – To delete an item from your set
- Set.clear() – To clear all items from your set

In the following example, we utilize all three methods to create a set that contains only the value 5 before clearing it to empty:

```
let mySet = new Set()
mySet.add(4)
mySet.add(5)
mySet.delete(4)
console.log(mySet) // Set(1) {5}
```

```
mySet.clear()
console.log(mySet) // Set(0) {}
```

Checking Set Membership

Since the main use case of sets is to create unique lists, they become a powerful tool for checking if a certain value exists in a specific set. Sets have a built-in method called Set.has() to do this:

```
let mySet = new Set()
mySet.add(4)
mySet.add(5)
mySet.delete(4)

let checkSet = mySet.has(4)
console.log(checkSet) // false
```

Checking Set Size

While in arrays we use Array.length to give us the size of an array, sets instead use a property called size to achieve the same functionality:

```
let mySet = new Set()
mySet.add(4)
mySet.add(5)
mySet.add(6)
console.log(mySet.size) // Console logs 3
```

Merging Sets

Since sets are iterable and implement the iterator protocol, they can be merged using the three dots operator (...), as shown in the following example. Duplicates will automatically be removed if any exist. You can see how this looks in Figure 9-1.

```
let mySetOne = new Set()
mySetOne.add(4)
mySetOne.add(5)
let mySetTwo = new Set()
mySetTwo.add(5)
let bigSet = new Set([...mySetOne, ...mySetTwo])
console.log(bigSet) // Set{2} {4, 5}
```

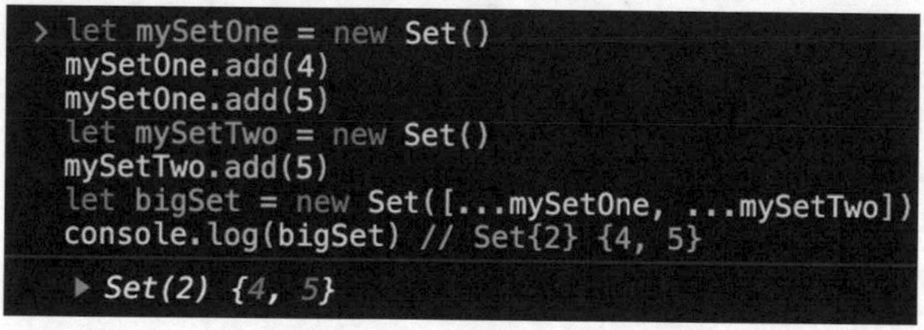

Figure 9-1. *Sets can be merged using the three dots syntax since they are iterable. By doing so, the new set will have all duplicates removed from it*

Set Iteration and Values

Since sets are iterable, meaning they can be fed into `for...of` loops as you would for arrays. However, using `for...in` loops will not work since sets do not have indices. Since sets do not have indexes, it also means you cannot access a set item with square bracket notation, like `mySet[2]`:

```
let mySet = new Set()
mySet.add(4)
mySet.add(5)
```

```
mySet.add(6)

for(let x of mySet) {
    console.log(x) // 4, 5, 6
}

for(let x in mySet) {
    console.log(x) // undefined
}
```

Just like arrays, sets also have a forEach method built in for easy iteration. As we've previously discussed, for loops are generally faster than using the forEach method, but they do have some advantages over a for loop such as creating a new context, since they use callback functions:

```
let mySet = new Set()
mySet.add(4)
mySet.add(5)
mySet.add(6)

mySet.forEach((x) => {
    console.log(x) // 4, 5, 6
})
```

Finally, if the limitations on set methods or their lack of indices become too much, you can easily convert a set to an array instead by using Array.from(). After that, you'll be able to use all array methods on your set:

```
let mySet = new Set()
mySet.add(4)
mySet.add(5)
mySet.add(6)

let arrayFromSet = Array.from(mySet) // [ 4, 5, 6 ]
```

Set Keys and Values

Just like objects, sets inherit keys(), values(), and entries() methods. In sets, both keys() and values() do the same thing and will simply return a list of all members in the set as a special object known as a SetIterator:

```
let mySet = new Set()
mySet.add(5)
mySet.add(10)
let getKeys = mySet.keys() // SetIterator{5, 10}
```

SetIterators are different from sets, and they only have one method, that being the method next(). The next() method allows you to iterate through sets one item at a time. Each time you do, an object is returned consisting of the value of the set item and whether iteration is complete. You can see what that looks like in the following example:

```
let mySet = new Set()
mySet.add(5)
mySet.add(10)
let getKeys = mySet.keys() // SetIterator{5, 10}
console.log(getKeys.next()) // { value: 5, done: false }
console.log(getKeys.next()) // { value: 10, done: false }
console.log(getKeys.next()) // { value: undefined,
done: false }
```

While keys() and values() provide a shorthand way to generate SetIterators, they can also be created by referring to the sets iterator property instead to achieve the same result:

```
let mySet = new Set()
mySet.add(5)
mySet.add(10)
let getKeys = mySet[Symbol.iterator]() // SetIterator{5, 10}
```

```
console.log(getKeys.next()) // { value: 5, done: false }
console.log(getKeys.next()) // { value: 10, done: false }
console.log(getKeys.next()) // { value: undefined,
done: false }
```

Note   You can also iterate through SetIterators using a for...of loop as they are iterable.

The entries() method is also available to all sets. On objects, the entries method returns arrays in the form [key, value]. Since sets do not have keys, the value is returned as both the key and the value.

The main reason why this method is available in sets is to ensure consistency with maps, which do have keys and values. Set.entries() still returns a SetIterator, just like keys() and values():

```
let mySet = new Set()
mySet.add(5)
mySet.add(10)
let setEntries = mySet.entries()

for(let x of setEntries) {
    console.log(x)
    // Returns [ 5, 5 ], [ 10, 10 ]
}
```

Maps

While sets are array-like structures that also provide automatic duplicate removal, maps are object-like structures with some additional enhancements. While similar to objects, they also differ in some very important ways:

- Maps have no prototype – While map objects do inherit a prototype, the map itself contains no keys unless we insert one into it. In JavaScript objects, we have to use `Object.hasOwnProperty()` to find out if a property is from the object itself or its prototype. Maps do not search the prototype, meaning we know maps will only have what we explicitly put into them, and will not inherit other properties.

- Maps guarantee order by chronology – They are guaranteed to be ordered by the order they were inserted. Since maps use a specific `set()` method to create new entries, the order of entries corresponds chronologically to when `set()` was used.

- Maps allow anything to be set as a key – The keys of a map can be anything, including a `Function` or even an `Object`. In objects, it must be a string or symbol.

- Maps have performance benefits – They have better performance than objects on tasks that require rapid or frequent removal/addition of data.

- Maps are iterable by default, unlike objects.

Similar to with sets, a map is initiated using the `new Map()` constructor:

```
let myMap = new Map()
```

And just like sets, maps come with `add()`, `delete()`, and `clear()` methods. The key difference here is that to add map items, you need to specify both a key and a value and to delete a map item, you have to specify the key name you wish to delete. You can see how these methods work in the following example and in Figure 9-2.

```
let myMap = new Map()
myMap.set("key", "value")
myMap.set("secondKey", "value")
```

```
myMap.delete("key")
console.log(myMap) // Map(1) {'secondKey' => 'value'}
myMap.clear()
console.log(myMap) // Map(0) {}
```

Figure 9-2. *Adding an entry to the* Map *using square bracket notation adds it to the object, at the same level as the prototype. It does not add an entry to the map itself, meaning you lose all the benefits of* Maps

Since it is not possible to set one key before another with set(), maps order is reliably assumed to be chronological.

Somewhat confusingly, maps seem to be able to have items set using the square bracket notation, but this is not the right way to set new map entries. In fact, setting a property on a map using square brackets results in the property being defined on the map object, and not in the map itself:

```
let myMap = new Map()
myMap.set("hello", "world")
myMap[0] = "hello"

console.log(myMap)
```

The separation between map entries set with the square bracket notation and the object containing the map is why maps do not inherit properties from a prototype. You can see this separation in Figure 9-3, where an [[Entries]] section exists to contain actual map entries, while the prototype and other properties are set on the map object itself.

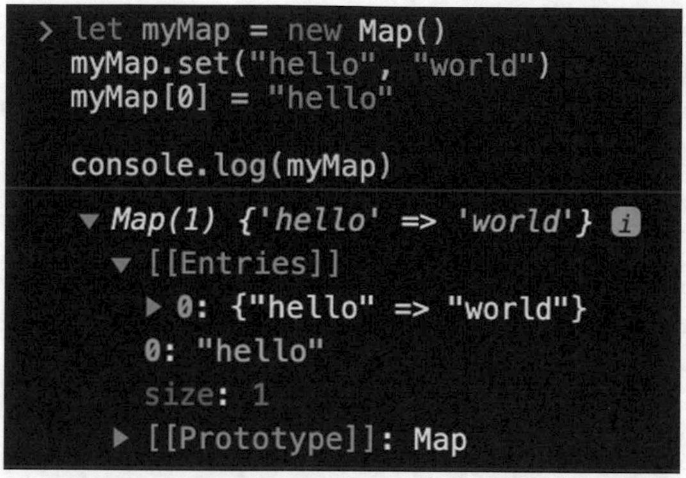

```
> let myMap = new Map()
  myMap.set("hello", "world")
  myMap[0] = "hello"

  console.log(myMap)

▼ Map(1) {'hello' => 'world'} ⓘ
  ▼ [[Entries]]
    ▶ 0: {"hello" => "world"}
    0: "hello"
    size: 1
  ▶ [[Prototype]]: Map
```

Figure 9-3. *Maps do not inherit a prototype since their properties are contained in a special property called [[Entries]]. Trying to set a property on the map itself with square brackets will not work since the property will be set in the map object*

While objects only allow strings, numbers, or symbols to be set as keys, maps allow keys to be of any type. As such, a function key is possible in maps while impossible in objects:

```
let myMap = new Map()
myMap.set(() => { return true }, "value")
console.log(myMap) // Map(1) {{f => 'value'}}
```

Retrieving Map Properties

To retrieve items from a map, we use a method called get():

```
let myMap = new Map()
myMap.set("key", "value")
myMap.set("secondKey", "value")

console.log(myMap.get("key"))
```

Since maps do not inherit prototypes, we do not run into key conflicts. For example, objects will typically inherit keys like valueOf() from their prototype. That means that we can use this method on any object, as is shown in the following example:

```
let myObject = { "key" : "value" }
myObject.valueOf() // Returns value of myObject
```

With maps, these methods are not inherited and thus will not exist. This prevents any chance of key conflict.

```
let myMap = new Map()
myMap.set("key", "value")
myMap.set("secondKey", "value")
console.log(myMap.get("myValue")) // undefined
```

Since maps can have keys of any type, retrieving nonprimitive keys can become a little tricky. To do that, we must mention the original reference to the key, meaning we need to store the key in a variable to reliably retrieve it. You can see how that works in the following example:

```
let myMap = new Map()
let someArray = [ 1, 2 ]
myMap.set(someArray, "value")
```

To retrieve the someArray entry, we reference the variable, someArray:

```
myMap.get(someArray) // value
```

The functionality that allows us to set map keys to any value leads to some interesting problems. Since the map holds a reference to the object, someArray, someArray will never be garbage collected. Normally, when objects become unreferenced, JavaScript will automatically remove them from memory.

This means that if you do what we did in the preceding example enough, you might run into memory issues, and ultimately memory *errors* in your code.

To overcome that particular problem, another type of map called a WeakMap exists. WeakMaps have a more limited set of methods (get, set, has, and delete) but will allow for garbage collection of objects where the only reference to that object is in the WeakMap. WeakMaps are not iterable, meaning accessing them relies solely on get(). This makes them much more limited than maps but useful when solving this particular problem. You can create a WeakMap in the same way as a map, but by using the WeakMap constructor instead:

```
let myMap = new WeakMap()
let someArray = [ 1, 2 ]
myMap.set(someArray, "value")
```

Checking for Key Existence on a Map

We can check for a key's membership on a map using the has() method:

```
let myMap = new Map()
myMap.set('firstKey', 'someValue')
myMap.has('firstKey') // true
```

Telling How Big a Javascript Map Is

Just like in sets, maps use the size property rather than length to get the number of keys that exist within them:

```
let myMap = new Map()
myMap.set('firstKey', 'someValue')
myMap.size // 1
```

This is actually an improvement upon `objects`. Since objects don't have a length by default, we typically use a mixture of `Object.keys()` to convert them to arrays in order to find their size:

```
let myObj = { "name" : "John" };
let sizeOfObj = Object.keys(myObj).length; // 1
Using Maps with non-string keys
```

Iterating, Merging, and Accessing Maps

Another useful feature of maps is the fact that they are iterable by default. Firstly, that means they can be merged using the three dots operator (...), as shown in the following example:

```
let myMapOne = new Map()
myMapOne.set("key", "value")
let myMapTwo = new Map()
myMapTwo.set("secondKey", "value")
// Map{2} {4, 5}
let bigMap = new Map([...myMapOne, ...myMapTwo])
console.log(bigMap) // Map(2) {'key' => 'value', 'secondKey' =>
'value'}
```

This is very different from objects, where we typically need to use `Object.keys()`, `Object.entries()`, or `Object.values()` to iterate through them

```
let myObject = { "item-1": false, "item-2": true,
"item-3": false }
let getKeys = Object.keys(myObject)
for(let item of getKeys) {
    console.log(myObject[item])
}
```

With maps, things are simpler. We can iterate straight on the map itself. When we do this with a `for...of` loop, this returns a handy key–value array item. We also have the option of using the built-in `forEach` method:

```
let myMap = new Map()
myMap.set("key", "value")
myMap.set("secondKey", "value")

for(let item of myMap) {
    console.log(item) // [ 'key', 'value' ], [ 'secondKey',
    'value' ]
    console.log(item[1]) // 'value', 'value'
}

myMap.forEach((x) => {
    console.log(x) // 'value', 'value'
})
```

Keys and Values in Maps

Maps also have `keys()`, `values()`, and `entries()` methods. All of these methods return a special type of object known as `MapIterator`. This is essentially the same as when we looked at sets, which returned a `SetIterator` for these methods.

Since object keys can only be symbols, numbers, or strings, usually we only use the key for accessing object values. However, in maps, keys can be of any type, so the `keys()` method takes on a more useful role in giving us the key value, which can actually be something useful like a function.

```
let myMap = new Map()
myMap.set("key", "value")
myMap.set("secondKey", "value")

let mapKeys = myMap.keys()
```

```
console.log(mapKeys.next()) // {value: 'key', done: false}
console.log(mapKeys.next()) // {value: 'secondKey',
done: false}
console.log(mapKeys.next()) // {value: undefined, done: true}
```

Note   MapIterators remain iterable, so you can use a for...of loop on them too.

The same functionality we have shown above for keys can be achieved for values too, using Map.values():

```
let myMap = new Map()
myMap.set("key", "value")
myMap.set("secondKey", "value")

let mapValues = myMap.values()
console.log(mapValues.next()) // {value: "value", done: false}
console.log(mapValues.next()) // {value: "value", done: false}
console.log(mapValues.next()) // {value: undefined, done: true}
```

Finally, we can retrieve both key and value in this format by using Map.entries(). It returns each key–value pair as [key, value]:

```
let myMap = new Map()
myMap.set("key", "value")
myMap.set("secondKey", "value")

let mapValues = myMap.entries()
console.log(mapValues.next()) // {value: [ "key", "value" ],
done: false}
console.log(mapValues.next()) // {value: [ "secondKey", "value"
], done: false}
console.log(mapValues.next()) // {value: undefined, done: true}
```

Serialization of Maps in JavaScript

When we want to serialize a JavaScript object, we use JSON.parse() and JSON.stringify(). Since maps are empty objects with entries within them, trying to stringify them results in an empty object string:

```
let myMap = new Map()
myMap.set("key", "value")
myMap.set("secondKey", "value")

console.log(JSON.stringify(myMap)) // "{}"
```

The only way to serialize a map for transfer over an API is to convert it to an object or array. To do that, we can use Array.from() to convert our map to an array and then use JSON.stringify() to serialize it:

```
let myMap = new Map()
myMap.set("key", "value")
myMap.set("secondKey", "value")
myMap.set("thirdKey", "value")

let objConversion = Array.from(myMap)
// Returns [["some","value"],["someOther","value"],["aFinal",
"value"]]
console.log(JSON.stringify(objConversion))
```

To change it back to a map, we can then use JSON.parse() in conjunction with new Map(). In this case, an array of entries passed into the map constructor will result in a fully formed map object:

```
let myMap = new Map()
myMap.set("key", "value")
myMap.set("secondKey", "value")
myMap.set("thirdKey", "value")
```

```
let objConversion = JSON.stringify(Array.from(myMap))
// Returns [["some","value"],["someOther","value"],["aFinal",
"value"]]
console.log(objConversion)

let toObj = JSON.parse(objConversion)
let toMap = new Map(toObj)
// Map(3) {'key' => 'value', 'secondKey' => 'value', 'thirdKey'
=> 'value'}
console.log(toMap)
```

Summary

In this chapter, we've covered sets and maps. We've gone over the utility of both and when you would use them over regular objects. Sets allow for unique lists, while maps have lots of extra utility that objects simply do not.

Up until this point, we've been relying entirely on objects and arrays to handle our data. Now you can be more specific and create sets and maps when the need arises too. Since these objects are optimized for the tasks we've described in this chapter, they can also provide additional optimization to your code.

CHAPTER 10

Fetching Data, APIs, and Promises

Throughout this book, we've made reference to APIs, but we haven't gone into detail about how they work. To put it simply, an API is a way for us to request and receive information from a computation process happening outside of your current application. This includes other computers and servers. API, which stands for **a**pplication **p**rogramming **i**nterface, provide a standard mechanism for sending and receiving this interaction. If you want to create things like login pages, user accounts, or persistent user data on the web, we usually use APIs. The reason we have to use something like an API for these things is because front end JavaScript is local to a user's computer, whereas SQL databases containing a user's email or password are usually stored on a server. Therefore it would be next to impossible to process all of this information on a front end JavaScript application in someone's browser due to security problems.

In this chapter, we'll cover how APIs work in JavaScript and go into detail about how best to utilize them. We'll also look at how to use the fetch() function, along with the associated Promise type, and learn about asynchronicity.

© Jonathon Simpson 2023
J. Simpson, *How JavaScript Works*, https://doi.org/10.1007/978-1-4842-9738-4_10

What Are APIs?

In simple terms, APIs provide a way to abstract complicated computation into simple calls we can process anywhere in our code. For example, imagine you want to build a piece of software which takes image data and then tells you which items exist in that image. Usually, the image processing part would be done through some kind of machine learning, while the image data may be uploaded via a web interface.

While implementing a way to upload images is relatively straight forward in front end JavaScript, adding in machine learning to process these uploaded images is a little more complex. Furthermore, doing this all on the front end would probably not be practical. For one, you probably don't want users to have to download this potentially quite complicated piece of software every time they visit your website, and secondly you might also want to write it in another language like Python. Furthermore, you may lack the knowledge to create this machine learning software effectively.

To solve these problems, it's usually preferable to create this piece of software on a server somewhere instead. We can then open up access to this software via API, allowing anyone to send image data to the server and receive back an array of items that exist in any given image. This approach to software development has two major advantages:

- The API can be maintained by someone who knows a lot about Python and machine learning. This means the quality of the code could be a lot higher than if everyone built their own machine learning algorithms.

- Even though the API is written in Python, as long as the response is sent via HTTP, it can still be interacted with from JavaScript.

In front end JavaScript development, we depend on back end APIs to enhance functionality and build more advanced capabilities into our websites, like login and registration systems. These back end APIs are often written in JavaScript too, but that's not always the case! All APIs on the Web are sent via HTTP, which is the same protocol you use to open any website in your browser. HTTP stands for **H**ypertext **T**ransfer **P**rotocol, and it's why URLs start with `http://` or `https://`.

Note   Sometimes, APIs don't just create an interface between two computers. Instead, they can create interfaces between your JavaScript code and your operating system. These are Web APIs. We'll go into these APIs in much more detail in the next chapter.

APIs on the Web commonly follow a set of design principles known as REST, so you may see these APIs referred to as REST APIs. REST stands for **representational state transfer** and refers to APIs implementing the following principles:

- They use HTTP to communicate between different computers (i.e., server and web page).

- They are stateless, meaning any API call with the same request will produce the same result.

- They are based around *resources* or *things*. For example: an article on a website is a *resource*, which we then *do* something with. For example, we can get an article, update the article, or delete the article.

- They are language agnostic, so our example Python API should still work even if the API request comes from JavaScript.

A simple representation of how APIs work can be found in Figure 10-1.

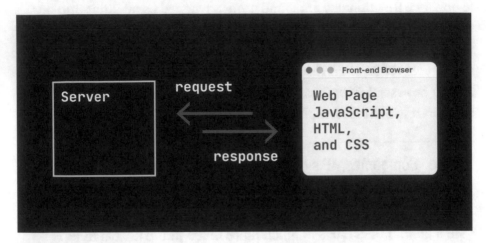

Figure 10-1. *APIs allow for communication between servers and web pages. Sometimes, APIs may be built into the browser and allow communication between the operating system and a web page, such as with Web APIs*

Understanding HTTP

Before we dig into the practicalities of creating APIs in JavaScript, let's learn more about HTTP. HTTP, and more commonly HTTPS, the *S* standing for secure, is the standard protocol for loading web pages on the Internet.

You can find out a little more about HTTP if you open your browser's console **Network** tab and then open any web page. This section will become populated with a lot of entries naming the things that this web page has loaded via HTTP. If you click one, you'll see something similar to Figure 10-2.

Name						
	×	**Headers**	Preview	Response	Initiator	Timing	Cookies

Name
- fjolt.com
- vue-v-show.webp
- js?id=G-5GH1XBD5WM
- carbon.js?serve=CESI5KJN&…
- inpageSol.js
- data:image/svg+xml;…

▼ General

Request URL:	https://fjolt.com/
Request Method:	GET
Status Code:	● 200
Remote Address:	109.228.53.122:443
Referrer Policy:	strict-origin-when-cross-origin

Figure 10-2. *Web pages are loaded via HTTP GET requests*

When connecting to a website via a browser, the browser sends an HTTP request to a domain, which ultimately points to the IP of a server or computer somewhere. A website may request more HTTP resources to load images, JavaScript files, and CSS files.

An HTTP request is ultimately a string of text, which your browser transmits to another computer. In typical terminology, we refer to the computer sending the request as the client and the computer receiving the request as the server. In the example shown in Figure 10-2, we are trying to connect to `fjolt.com` which points to a server with the IP `109.228.53.122:433`.

For HTTP to work, the server needs to be configured correctly to receive HTTP requests. This can be done by setting up an Apache or Node. JS web server. If that is done correctly, then the HTTP server interprets the HTTP request and sends back a *response* to the client computer.

With APIs, we can tell the server to do certain things whenever someone tries to go to a specific URL on that server. These different URLs, in the context of APIs, are commonly referred to as **routes** or **endpoints**.

In summary, all HTTP requests and therefore all APIs have two parts:

- The `request`, which contains the string of information from you, your browser, or your code, about what you want from the server.

- The `response`, which contains the reply from the server.

227

To expose how simple an HTTP request can be, here is the HTTP request for a made-up website called some-website.org, from a browser with the user agent Mozilla/5.0. User agent here refers to the unique string which identifies each browser. In simple terms, all this is doing is creating a request with some specific instructions which a server will then interpret. If the server is set up to accept HTTP requests, it will send a response:

```
GET /page HTTP/1.1
Host: some-website.org
User-Agent: Mozilla/5.0
Connection: Keep-Alive
```

Note   To get your own IP and domain, you have to use a web host. A web host will usually give you a server with a specific IP and a domain. There are plenty of options for this available online. You can then host .html, .css and .js files directly on this web server or use it as a location to spin up a Node.JS web server instead.

RESTful Design

Earlier, we described how most APIs are based around RESTful design principles. APIs are also usually designed to request specific resources. In the context of APIs, a resource could refer to anything. For example, in the context of web development, this could refer to an image, article, category of content, or comment on an article.

These concepts also extend to navigation on the web itself, where the web page itself is the resource, and the browser performs a request to retrieve its contents. Each time an HTTP request is sent, it comes with a specific action keyword. For example, opening a web page performs the GET HTTP method.

Each of these actions come with expected behaviour. For example, when using GET, the expected behavior is that the server will return a resource. For web pages, this could mean returning HTML, but it's also pretty common for a web page URL to return XML or JSON too. GET is not the only type of HTTP request we can send, though. The other methods are shown below:

- GET – Meant for getting a resource

- POST – Generally meant for creating a new resource

- PUT – Meant for replacing entire resources or major parts of resources

- PATCH – Meant for modifying small parts of a resource

- DELETE – Meant for deleting resources

- CONNECT – Meant for initial connection to the URL or IP. Usually used when there is encryption or authentication required

- TRACE – Meant for looping back the response as the request, for testing purposes

While a web page (or resource) is normally retrieved via a GET request, using DELETE on it instead will usually result in the resource being deleted instead. We usually add authentication to these more dangerous methods so that users can't randomly delete important content.

Note   In the context of API design, you may see the acronym CRUD. This stands for Create, Read, Update, Delete, which are the actions a RESTful API may perform on a resource. These actions are implemented via POST, GET, PUT/PATCH, and DELETE, respectively.

In summary, when we open a web page, what's really happening is the browser is sending a GET HTTP request to a server, and the server is sending back the web page as a response. If it's a normal web page, the response body will contain the HTML, JavaScript, and CSS for that website. Some URLs may return other data types like JSON or XML instead. Your browser then loads that into its viewport, and that's what you see.

If you could change how your web browser worked so that it always sent POST requests instead of GET, the web would look very different. Trying to access Google, for example, would throw a 405 error. For other websites, you might receive other responses, or you might end up posting and creating new data on a server somewhere instead! That's because although you are visiting the same websites, each HTTP method is configured to act differently. Therefore, the HTTP method we use is important when using APIs and navigating the web.

Understanding APIs Through a Node.JS Web Server

Now that we've explored HTTP in a little bit of depth, let's look at the practicalities around how APIs work. To understand how this works fully, we're going to have to get a little familiar with Node.js, and how it can be used to create a web server.

Node.js is an implementation of JavaScript which works mostly in the same way browser JavaScript does, except Node.js applications run on servers or directly on computers. It is common in Node.js to import libraries of software from an online repository of projects called npmjs. org in order to provide additional functionality to our own code.

Note   A web server is created on a specific port. It waits for connections to hit a specific URL or endpoint with an HTTP request and then responds to the person, browser, or computer initiating the connection (the client) before sending a response back.

To start to understand how APIs work, let's create a Node.js web server. Before you begin, make sure to install Node.js from nodejs.org. This will also include access to npmjs.org and the npm terminal tools. For the purposes of this exercise, you can make a new folder anywhere on your computer and call it "node-server."

Start by creating a file called app.js in that folder with the following content:

```
const express = require("express")
const http = require("http")

let app = express()

let server = http.createServer(app)

app.get("/some/url", (request, response) => {
    // Do Something
    response.send("Hello World")
})

app.post("/some/url", (request, response) => {
    // Do Something
    response.send("Goodbye World")
})

server.listen(3000)
```

Let's explore what is going on here. In this example, we import two libraries called `http` and `express` using a built-in Node.js global function called `require()`. This function searches for a folder called `node_modules` in the same directory as your file and then loads the appropriate third party module into your code. Both of these libraries contain specific code which will let us create a web server.

The `http` library lets us make the HTTP server itself, which is what we'll need to create an API. Meanwhile, the `express` library lets us configure endpoints (or URLs) on that server, so that we have URLs to connect to. How these libraries work under the hood is not super important, but since the code for these libraries is open source, you can explore that in your own time online or in the `node_modules` folder. The `http` library, for example, can be found at `npmjs.com/package/http`.

Importing these libraries into our code is not enough to make them work. We also need to install them. To do that, navigate to your `node-server` folder (using `cd node-server` from terminal), and then run the following two commands to install `express` and `http`. You can see how this works in Figure 10-3.

```
npm i http
npm i express
```

Note   `require()` is a Node.JS global method. A standardized alternative called `import` is also available in Node.JS but requires you to convert your Node.JS project to a "module." This is easily achieved by either updating the package.json by adding `"type"`: `"module"` at the top level or by using the `.mjs` file extension instead of `.js`.

```
Last login: Sun Sep 10 16:27:51 on ttys005
johnnysimpson@Johnnys-MacBook-Pro ~ % cd ~/Documents/node-server
johnnysimpson@Johnnys-MacBook-Pro node-server % npm i http

up to date, audited 62 packages in 1s

8 packages are looking for funding
  run `npm fund` for details

found 0 vulnerabilities
npm notice
npm notice New major version of npm available! 9.8.1 -> 10.1.0
npm notice Changelog: https://github.com/npm/cli/releases/tag/v10.1.0
npm notice Run npm install -g npm@10.1.0 to update!
npm notice
johnnysimpson@Johnnys-MacBook-Pro node-server % npm i express
```

Figure 10-3. *Once Node.JS is installed, you can use terminal to install dependencies via the npm command*

Now that we've installed our packages, let's look at the rest of the code found in app.js. First, we use express to create the available URLs on the web server:

```
app.get("/some/url", (request, response) => {
```

app.get("/some/url"..., can be summarized as saying that when someone tries to GET "/some/url" on this server, then Node.js should run a specific callback function. In this case, the callback function generates a response saying "Hello World":

```
app.get("/some/url", (request, response) => {
    // Do Something
    response.send("Hello World")
})
```

In the callback function body which we define in this request, we have access to both the request sent by the user (along with all the HTTP request details that the client sends to us) and also the response, which we can use to send something back to the client via the `response.send()` method. If the user navigates to "/some/url" on this server, then the response they receive will be whatever we define in this send function.

If we plan to send HTML to the user, we can change our response to do that. This is used in something known as server-side rendering (SSR), which is a very efficient way to serve HTML to users. Sending HTML files can be done with the `sendFile` method in express, as shown in the following example, where we send a file called "index.html":

```
app.get("/some/url", (request, response) => {
    // Do Something
    response.sendFile("./index.html", { root: __dirname })
})
```

In app.js, we have also configured a POST request, which sends a response to the user if they try to post to the same URL ("/some/url"). This time, it sends "Goodbye World" as a response:

```
app.post("/some/url", (request, response) => {
    // Do Something
    response.send("Goodbye World")
})
```

Express supports all of the HTTP methods we described earlier, and while we've only sent responses here, we could also configure these endpoints to do something else with the request data, like store it in a database.

Note   It's relatively common for a server to store data it receives via a POST API request. For example, there are Node.JS packages for MySQL and MongoDB which allow you to save data sent to the server in the server's database. You could also store user data from a registration form, letting you create login systems.

To finish app.js, we attach these endpoints to the HTTP server we plan to set up. To do that we use two lines of code - one which creates the server from the express app and another which listens on port 3000 for connections:

```
let server = http.createServer(app)
// ...
server.listen(3000)
```

Once our file is complete, we can run it by using the terminal or command line. To do that, we use a command called node. If you saved this file as app.js, then the following line of code in the terminal will start your web server:

```
node app.js
```

Most computers have localhost set up to point to their local IP (127.0.0.1). If that's the case for your computer, going to localhost:3000/some/url in your browser should bring up the Node.js server we just set up. Since our server was set up to send "Hello World" when using the GET command on this URL, you should see the text "Hello World" in your browser. If localhost is not set up on your computer, you may have to navigate to 127.0.0.1:3000/some/url instead.

Note   When running node app.js, the app.js file will only run as long as the terminal session persists. To ensure a web server continuously runs for as long as the computer or server is switched on, it's pretty common to install a production command instead. One commonly used production command is pm2. You can install it by running npm install pm2 -g and then permanently start up your web server by running pm2 start app.js.

Testing Endpoints with Postman

Now that we have a server running in the background, we'll want to be able to easily access the endpoints we've set up on it. This is particularly useful when we want to test code. A useful tool for testing web servers like this is **Postman**. You can download it via <u>postman.com</u>. Postman lets you use any HTTP method to request certain endpoints/URLs. It also has useful tools for authentication should your APIs implement that. You can see what Postman looks like in Figure 10-4.

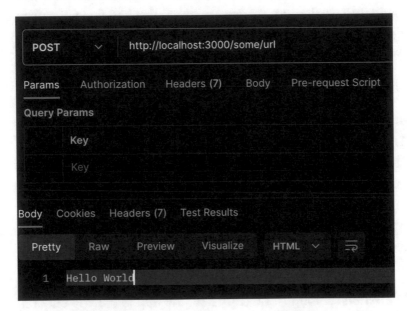

Figure 10-4. *Postman lets you test out any endpoint responses from any public URL. When our web server is running on port 3000, it lets us easily test responses from it*

The Benefits of APIs

APIs can be called from anywhere in JavaScript as is illustrated in Figure 10-5. They can be called as soon as the page loads, but more commonly they are triggered when the user does something. For example, if a user clicks "Login," an API could send their login credentials for verification to the server. This user-facilitated API call can be done via .addEventListener(), which we covered in a previous chapter.

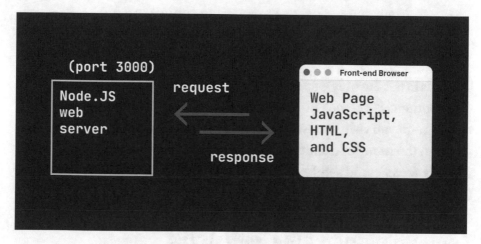

Figure 10-5. *APIs can be interacted with from anywhere, but in web development, the requests are usually sent from the front end to the back end via a JavaScript method called* fetch. *Requests and responses usually take the form of JSON*

Using APIs in your applications has two major benefits which we haven't discussed yet:

- The server takes on the computation load – While this is not a big deal for things like user login, it can become more important for complex computation. For example, imagine if the server was a supercomputer, which could tell you the weather at any pinpoint location. On a user's computer, such a calculation may be impossible, but the supercomputer can do this for us and then send us the response via API.

- It allows us to build microservices – Using APIs, we can create reusable code based on RESTful principles. We can deploy these APIs independently of the rest of our code, allowing us to version control specific functionality. For example, we could have separate APIs for login, registration, status updates, and so on.

This is not the only way servers and APIs can be used in web development. Since web browsers trigger a GET HTTP request to any URL or endpoint you visit, some servers are configured to serve entire web pages to the user. For example, configuring the endpoint GET /home on a Node.js server could send a response to the user where the response is the HTML for the home page.

Sending Data to APIs with JSON

When we send data to APIs in JavaScript, it's usually sent in the form of JSON, which stands for **JavaScript Object Notation.**

A JSON object, for the most part, just looks like a regular JavaScript object. An example of one is shown below:

```
{
    "name" : "John",
    "age" : 105,
    "interests" : [ "hiking", "skiing", "working" ]
}
```

To work with JSON, a top-level global object called JSON exists. This contains two static methods for managing JSON:

- JSON.stringify() for serializing JSON into a string (i.e. turning a JSON object into a string).

- JSON.parse() for turning a string consisting of JSON back into a functioning JSON object.

When sending data to an endpoint (e.g., if we want to POST data to a Node.js web server), we usually send it as stringified JSON:

```
JSON.stringify({
    "name" : "John",
    "age" : 105,
    "interests" : [ "hiking", "skiing", "working" ]
})

/*
This will return a string:
'{"name":"John","age":105,"interests":["hiking","skiing",
"working"]}'
*/
```

To turn this back into a JavaScript object, we use JSON.parse():

```
JSON.parse('{"name":"John","age":105,"interests":["hiking",
"skiing","working"]}')

/* This will return an object:
{
    "name" : "John",
    "age" : 105,
    "interests" : [ "hiking", "skiing", "working" ]
}
*/
```

These methods are typically used before we send data to an API and then when we receive it. For example, before we send JSON data to an endpoint on a server, we would typically stringify it. Then, on the server side, we'd parse it to get the JavaScript JSON object back again.

While JSON can be considered almost identical to any normal JavaScript object, there are some differences. When you try to stringify or parse an object into JSON, you will encounter these limitations:

- undefined, Function, and Symbol do not work in JSON. These properties will disappear when using JSON.stringify or JSON.parse.

- Maps or sets (two data types we'll cover in a later chapter) are parsed to {} in JSON.

- Dates are parsed to strings since Date has a .toJSON method.

- Infinity, NaN, and null are all considered null.

The fetch Function

So far, we've only looked at how we can set up an API server. Now that we've covered how APIs work and why we use them, let's look at how we can create API connections in JavaScript. The fetch() method is the function we use on the front end to send requests to a server. It exists on the global window object, so running fetch() at the top level by itself will work. At its simplest, fetch will hit a URL with a GET HTTP request and then wait for a response from the server. This is best illustrated by the following example:

```
fetch("https://google.com").then((res) => {
    // Do something with response
})
```

As we discussed earlier, when we request a URL, a response is sent back. Using the fetch function, we initiate a request, which then generates a response. The response (or res), can only be accessed inside then() in this example. You might be wondering why we have to use then() along with the fetch function, and that's a good question!

The reason why is simple. When we try to request a URL, it takes some time for the URL to load, run the server code it needs to, and then send a response back to us. Since JavaScript works via the stack, the fetch function will be run, but JavaScript will just move on to the next item in the stack and never wait for a response.

For this reason, the fetch function returns a special type of data which is known as a `Promise`. It's called that because `fetch()` is promising to us that a response will eventually be generated. When we use `then()`, it waits for the promise to generate a response. When it does, it will run the code inside the `then()` function's body. The response from the `Promise` is stored in the `res` variable. In the previous example, we used `then()` on a fetch request, but it can actually be used on any `Promise`.

If you try to console log the `res` variable, you'll eventually get the response object containing data about the response from the server. The `res.body` property contains the main body of the response sent by the server, while res contains other details about the response. The response is of type `ReadableStream`, which is the standard transferable object type in JavaScript.

In this `ReadableStream` form, it's not very useful to us, so to convert our response into usable data, we have five methods attached to every HTTP response:

- `res.text()` – Takes the HTTP response body and returns the text content of its response. If it's a website, for example, it returns the HTML.

- `res.json()` – Takes the HTTP response body and returns formatted JSON data if it exists.

- `res.blob()` – Takes the HTTP response body and returns formatted blob data (usually binary data for an image or video) if any exists.

- `res.arrayBuffer()` – Takes the HTTP response body and returns a formatted `arrayBuffer`, if one exists.

- `res.formData()` – Takes the HTTP response body and returns `formData`, if any exists.

To illustrate this, imagine our API returns HTML data. We can use `res.text()` to change our body from a `ReadableStream` to actual, usable HTML:

```
fetch("https://google.com").then((res) => {
    // this parses the response as text
    return res.text()
}).then((data) => {
    // we can now access the raw HTML of the web page via data
})
```

In a similar vein, if our URL returns JSON, `res.json()` gives us the JSON object which we can parse as a regular JavaScript object:

```
fetch("http://localhost:3000/some/api").then((res) => {
    // when fetch is received, jsonObject will become the
parsed JSON version of the response.
    return res.json()
}).then((data) => {
    // Once received and parsed, we can now access our response
as JSON.
    let jsonData = data
})
```

In summary, we can request any URL or API using the fetch function in JavaScript. This function returns a special type of data known as a "promise". We can wait for a promise to resolve into a response by using a function called "then". Now that we understand these basics, let's look at how we can customize our fetch requests.

A Deep Dive into Fetch Options

So far, we've described how HTTP requests can be configured to have different HTTP methods, like GET and POST. HTTP requests can be further configured with other settings and headers, which allow us to modify how the request is sent.

When you are sending HTTP requests, you'll find that most use cases only require the properties body, method, and headers. In the following section, we'll discuss all of the different properties which are available to you in the "fetch" function. Some of these are quite complicated, and if you're starting out it's not necessary to understand them all in graphic detail. In most scenarios, you'll really only want to send data (e.g. the "body"), via some HTTP method (e.g. the "method").

To illustrate all of the properties at your disposal, here is an example of a fetch function with all possible options configured:

```
fetch("https://google.com/", {
    body: JSON.stringify({ someData: "value" })
    mode: 'cors',
    method: 'POST',
    cache: 'no-cache',
    credentials: 'same-origin',
    referrer: 'some-site.com',
    headers: {
      'Content-Type': 'application/json'
    },
    redirect: 'follow',
    integrity: 'sha512-12345',
    keepalive: false,
    referrerPolicy: 'no-referrer'
});
```

A description of each can be found in the following section.

body

The body property is the main data you send to the web server. For example, we might send a stringified JSON object to the server via the body. Then, on the server, the body is parsed in order to do some calculations with it. In the previous example, we saw how we could send data via the fetch function in the body property. You can see what the corresponding server code might look like in the following example:

```
// Note: we use an express middleware here, called
// express.json(). It automatically parses all request bodies
// as JSON so we don't have to.
app.post("/some/url", express.json(), (request, response) => {
    let generateResponse = `You sent: ${request.body?.
    someData}`
    response.send(generateResponse)
})
```

mode

This property is used for configuring how cross-origin requests are handled. The possible options for this property are cors, no-cors, same-origin, navigate or websocket. Ultimately, this property will determine if cross-origin requests (i.e., requests between two different domains) are successful. If you try to send a request to a different domain (e.g., you are on localhost, and try to send a request to google.com), then you will get an error unless you set this to no-cors.

method

We have already discussed HTTP methods throughout this chapter. This property is where you can set the HTTP method you want to use. It can be set to POST, GET, DELETE, PUT, CONNECT, PATCH, TRACE or OPTION.

On the server, we can configure HTTP methods as well. In the following example, we configure a "put" method function:

```
app.put("/some/url", (request, response) => {})
```

cache

This property handles how caching works for this fetch request. It can be set to default, no-cache, reload, force-cache or only-if-cached. When you make an HTTP request, it is cached and reused to save time. By changing this setting to force-cache or another setting, you can change the default behavior so that the cache is never used.

credentials

Especially when configuring login systems, it is possible that the server will send a cookie back to you to store a session. Cookies are sensitive information, so it is useful to have a property which configures if the cookies are visible on the response. By changing this to include, the cookie will be saved. The possible values for this property are include, same-origin or omit.

headers

Headers are additional data points about the HTTP request which can tell the server to do specific things. Some headers are standard, and servers will interpret them in a specific way – like Cache-Control or Expires. which control aspects of caching. Other headers are custom. You can make any header you like, and it can add additional context about the kind of request you are trying to send.

redirect

This property determines what happens if the fetched URL redirects.

It can be set to `follow`, `error` or `manual`.

`follow` is the default value, and error will result in an HTTP error code. if you use `manual`, it will result in the HTTP response having a property called "type" which will be set to `opaqueredirect`, (res.type = "opaqueredirect"), allowing you to manually process what should happen on the client side.

referrer

When you send a request, the response will have a referrer header. By default, the referrer header is the URL you sent the request from. You can set a custom referrer via this property, as long as it's on the same domain as the fetch request. You can also set it as a blank string to show nothing.

referrerPolicy

Since the referrer is the URL you sent the request from, it can sometimes make sense to hide this information for security reasons. The `referrerPolicy` determines how much referrer information is passed with the request. Usually, you won't need to use this, but if you want to remove the `referrer` from the response for security reasons, this can be quite useful.

It can be set to one of the following:

- `no-referrer` – No referrer is sent.

- `no-referrer-when-downgrade` – No referrer is sent if you are sending from HTTPS to HTTP.

- `origin` – Only sends the domain, and not the URL, that is, some-site.com instead of some-site.com/some/page.

- `origin-when-cross-origin` – Only sends the domain if the request is cross-origin (different domains).

- `same-origin` – Only send the referrer if on the same domain.

- `strict-origin` – Sends only the origin for HTTPS to HTTP requests and the whole thing for HTTPS to HTTPS requests.

- `strict-origin-when-cross-origin` – Sends only the origin when HTTPS to HTTP requests or when cross-origin. Otherwise, it sends the referrer.

- `unsafe-url` – Always sends the referrer even if it's HTTPs to HTTP.

integrity

This special property is used to validate a subresource integrity (SRI). For example, a URL can be given a SRI value, which conforms to some cryptographic standard like SHA-256, SHA-384, or SHA-512. When we request it via fetch, we can set integrity to the expected SRI value for the resource we are requesting. If they match, it works. If it does not, then you'll get an error instead.

As an example, if you knew that the resource had an SRI value of 12345, and it had been encrypted with SHA-512, you would set integrity like so:

```
{ integrity: 'sha512-12345' }
```

keepalive

When you close a page, all requests are automatically aborted. Sometimes, this is not helpful. For example, if we were making an analytics tool that recorded precisely how long a page was open for, we'd never get that data back to the server. By setting keepalive, we can create a fetch request that will outlive the page's life cycle. The major limitation to this is you will not be able to process the response, and you can only fetch up to 64kb.

In summary, a fetch request can either be quite simple (requesting a single page via GET), or it can be made quite complicated with additional options. Not all of these options are required, and for everyday use, you won't need them. However, as you get deeper into JavaScript, you will find reasons to use all of them.

Asynchronicity and Promises

As we mentioned in the previous section, a fetch() request will return a Promise. This is a special type of object which makes a promise to us that a response will eventually be generated.

The fetch method is just one example of a function that requires time to process. That's because when we request an HTTP resource, we need to load that resource, download it, and wait for the response. To handle promises in the previous section, we used then(). This kind of behaviour is called asynchronous, since the code is not paused while the response is being generated.

```
let fetchExample = fetch("/some/api").then((res) => {
    return res.json()
}).then((data) => {
    let jsonData = data
})
```

If you don't use then(), and try to console log a fetch request, you'll find the raw Promise instead, which will read "Promise {<pending>}" on the console log.

```
let getData = fetch('/api/getData', { method: 'GET' })
console.log(getData) // Promise {<pending>}
```

Remember   If you get stuck in JavaScript, try console logging! If you console log `Promise.prototype`, you'll find a few useful hints on how it works. It contains the methods `then`, `finally`, and `catch`.

We can generate our own promises by using `Promise` as a constructor. Here is an example where we use two `setTimeout()` functions to do something after 1 and 1.5 seconds

```
let myPromise = new Promise((resolve, reject) => {
    setTimeout(function() {
        resolve(true)
    }, 1000)
    setTimeout(function() {
        reject(false)
    }, 1500)
})
```

Promise constructors accept a function with two arguments – usually called `resolve` and `reject`. Both of these arguments are functions.

In simple terms, if a promise is resolved, it is successful. If it is rejected, then an error is thrown. The return value is whatever is in the brackets of the `resolve` or `reject` function. Since we wrote `resolve(true)`, and this is the first `resolve`/`reject` function to fire, then the return value of this promise will simply be "true". If instead we'd written `resolve({ "someData" : true})`, the return result would've been `{ "someData" : true }`.

```
resolve(true)
// ...
reject(false)
```

Promise Methods: then, finally, and catch

Note   If a promise is rejected, we have to use `catch()` to see its contents rather than `then()`!

All promises have three methods attached to them, much like all objects and strings have certain methods we can apply to them. These methods are `then`, `finally`, and `catch`. You might find developers saying that promises are `thenable` because you can always apply a `then()` method to them. All three of these methods return a `Promise`, too, allowing you to chain a never-ending sequence of promises.

In our first example, we used then to catch the promise and return its data once the promise was resolved:

```
fetch("/some/api").then((res) => {
    return res.json()
}).then((data) => {
    let jsonData = data
})
```

The response of the `fetch` `Promise` is passed into the `res` variable, which we can then parse as JSON using `res.json()`. The reason why we can chain another "true" function is because `then()` always returns a promise, meaning we can catch this new promise in another `then()` function.

We can apply the same thought process to our previous example where we used `setTimeout()` too:

```
let myPromise = new Promise((fulfill, reject) => {
    setTimeout(function() {
        fulfill(true)
    }, 1000)
```

```
    setTimeout(function() {
        reject(false)
    }, 1500)
})

myPromise.then((response) => {
    console.log(response) // Console logs true
})
```

catch and finally

Now that we've looked at then(), let's look at the two other methods we have at our disposal when working with promises. These are catch() and finally().

If a promise is rejected, "catch" can be used to catch the error generated by that rejection and do something useful with it. This gives us a useful way to create a path for errors in our promises. You will find this particularly useful if a requested URL is expected to error out sometimes. For example, we could console some error logs if an API fails, rather than generating an actual error:

```
fetch("/some/api").then((res) => {
    return res.json()
}).then((data) => {
    let jsonData = data
}).catch((err) => {
    console.log("We ran into an issue")
    console.log(`Error: ${err}`)
})
```

When a promise is fully resolved, meaning the final promise in a chain resolves to be fulfilled or rejected, then we can use finally() to do any final housekeeping.

The main use case for finally is to perform any final steps after a promise is done. For example, we could show something to the user on their screen, once an API has fired:

```
fetch("/some/api").then((res) => {
    return res.json()
}).then((data) => {
    let jsonData = data
}).finally(() => {
    // Show #final-dialogue to user
    document.getElementById("final-dialogue").display = "block"
})
```

The await Keyword

While then() is a staple for processing promises, it does have some limitations. For example, we can only access the results of a promise inside a then() function. This causes problems if we want to use the result of a promise elsewhere in our code.

If we want to wait for a promise to be fully parsed without needing to use a then() function, we can use the await keyword instead. This lets us keep promises in line with other code, but it has the downside of pausing execution of the rest of the code until the promise is fulfilled. For example, given an API that returns { someData: "value" }, we can wait for a response before parsing that data using this method:

```
let getApi = await fetch("/some/api")
let result = getApi.someData // "value"
```

Additionally, if you find yourself needing to use await inside a function, you need to make the function **async**. Using the await keyword inside functions is usually recommended since await will only pause execution of that particular function, and not the entire JavaScript code. Here is the same example from before, now running inside a function instead:

```
let getApiFunction = async function() {
    let getApi = await fetch("/some/api")
    let result = getApi.someData // "value"
}

getApiFunction()
```

Originally, JavaScript only allowed await usage inside async functions. Nowadays, most JavaScript engines also support await at the top level of your application too.

If a promise is rejected and you use await instead of then()/catch(), then a regular error is thrown in JavaScript, but you can catch that in a try...catch expression instead.

Note   await and then both have valuable uses. Deciding which to use will depend on the structure of your code and how long APIs will take to deliver. You don't want to suspend all of your code due to a slow API, but you may always need to wait for some APIs before doing anything – like checking if a user is logged in via a login API.

Useful Promise Methods

There are four more really useful asynchronous promise methods that you should also know about. These are used for processing multiple promises at once. They are listed below:

- Promise.race – Which will return the promise which finishes first, when given multiple promises.

- Promise.allSettled – Which will wait for all promises to finish when given multiple promises and then return all promises as an array (whether they were rejected or fulfilled). The order of the array is the order the promises finished in.

- Promise.all – Which will wait for all promises to finish when given multiple promises and return all promises in an array, in the order they finished. If any promise is rejected, then it will return only the rejected promise. This differs from Promise.allSettled, which returns all promises, regardless of whether they were fulfilled or rejected.

- Promise.any – Which returns one promise, whichever one finishes first.

All of these methods can be used with await, but the following examples use then() and catch() instead. They all take arrays of promises as input. The arrays can take as many promises as you like. They also all return a Promise, letting you chain more promises onto them.

Promise.allSettled

Promise.allSettled waits for all promises in an array to finish before producing a new Promise with the results from all of those promises:

```
let firstPromise = new Promise((resolve, reject) =>
setTimeout(function() { resolve("Hello World") }, 1000))

let secondPromise = new Promise((resolve, reject) =>
setTimeout(function() { resolve("Not Sure World") }, 500))

let thirdPromise = new Promise((resolve, reject) =>
setTimeout(function() { reject("Goodbye World") }, 200))

Promise.allSettled([firstPromise, secondPromise,
thirdPromise]).then((data) => {
    console.log(data)
})
```

In the previous example, we have three promises, of which two resolve and another rejects. When they all finish, the output is the following:

```
{
    { status: 'fulfilled', value: 'Hello World' }
    { status: 'fulfilled', value: 'Not Sure World' }
    { status: 'rejected', reason: 'Goodbye World' }
}
```

When using any other method, you will get only the final value of the Promise, making Promise.allSettled() different in the way it returns Promise outcomes.

Promise.all

Promise.all() only returns one final outcome, for example, in the following code:

```
let firstPromise = new Promise((resolve, reject) =>
setTimeout(function() { resolve("Hello World") }, 1000))

let secondPromise = new Promise((resolve, reject) =>
setTimeout(function() { resolve("Not Sure World") }, 500))

let thirdPromise = new Promise((resolve, reject) =>
setTimeout(function() { resolve("Goodbye World") }, 200))

Promise.all([firstPromise, secondPromise, thirdPromise]).
then((data) => {
    console.log(data)
})
```

The final output here is as follows:

```
['Hello World', 'Not Sure World', 'Goodbye World']
```

If one promise had rejected, you would have to catch it using `catch()`, and only the rejected promise would come back:

```
let firstPromise = new Promise((resolve, reject) =>
setTimeout(function() { resolve("Hello World") }, 1000))

let secondPromise = new Promise((resolve, reject) =>
setTimeout(function() { resolve("Not Sure World") }, 500))

let thirdPromise = new Promise((resolve, reject) =>
setTimeout(function() { reject("Goodbye World") }, 200))

Promise.all([firstPromise, secondPromise, thirdPromise]).
catch((data) => {
    console.log(data)
})
```

The preceding code would simply return, "Goodbye World."

Promise.race

`Promise.race()` accepts an array of promises, too, and the fastest promise is returned. Using our previous examples, "Goodbye World" is fastest so using `Promise.race()` here returns the string, "Goodbye World":

```
let firstPromise = new Promise((resolve, reject) =>
setTimeout(function() { resolve("Hello World") }, 1000))

let secondPromise = new Promise((resolve, reject) =>
setTimeout(function() { resolve("Not Sure World") }, 500))

let thirdPromise = new Promise((resolve, reject) =>
setTimeout(function() { resolve("Goodbye World") }, 200))
```

```
Promise.race([firstPromise, secondPromise, thirdPromise]).
then((data) => {
    console.log(data)
})
```

Promise.any

Promise.any is a lot like Promise.race – it returns the value of the first promise to fulfill. The major difference is that Promise.race will return the first Promise which rejects or fulfills, while Promise.any will return only the first promise that fulfills. For example, even though thirdPromise is faster than secondPromise, Promise.any will return secondPromise as the final value since thirdPromise rejects:

```
let firstPromise = new Promise((resolve, reject) =>
setTimeout(function() { resolve("Hello World") }, 1000))

let secondPromise = new Promise((resolve, reject) =>
setTimeout(function() { resolve("Not Sure World") }, 500))

let thirdPromise = new Promise((resolve, reject) =>
setTimeout(function() { reject("Goodbye World") }, 200))

Promise.any([firstPromise, secondPromise, thirdPromise]).
then((data) => {
    console.log(data)
})
```

Promise.any then does something different if all promises reject. In this scenario, it returns a specific error type called an AggregateError. We can use catch() to catch this error:

```
Uncaught (in promise) AggregateError: All promises were
rejected
```

Summary

In this chapter, we've covered a lot of key concepts relating to APIs and asynchronous behavior in this chapter. At the beginning, we looked at how HTTP requests work. We then went into some detail about how we can create our own HTTP requests, and the key concepts behind RESTful design. After that, we looked at how we can create our own servers in Node.js and how these can be used to receive HTTP requests which we send on the front end via the fetch() function. Since fetch() is asynchronous, we've also gone into detail about how promises work, which is the type of object returned for asynchronous responses in JavaScript. Finally, we looked at how we can process promises using keywords and other functions.

Asynchronous behavior is really important in JavaScript since JavaScript's architecture means it doesn't automatically wait for the response from an asynchronous action before continuing in its execution of code. As such, having a strong grasp of these concepts is useful as you start to build your own applications. As such, the different promise methods we've covered in this chapter are vital to building modern web applications.

CHAPTER 11

Introduction to Web APIs

Writing JavaScript in the browser means that a lot of what we can do is limited by what the browser *allows* us to do. While core JavaScript functionality lets us create functions, math, and variables, what if, for example, we want to use the operating system's notification system from our code? Or store something locally on the user's computer? For each of these, JavaScript in the browser implements various Web APIs to allow programmers to access this functionality.

We've actually already encountered two of these APIs, that being the *HTML DOM document API* for query selecting HTML DOM elements and the *fetch API* for creating HTTP requests. In this chapter, we'll go over Web APIs in more detail and look at some very important ones.

Web APIs

In the previous chapter, we looked at how JavaScript can be used to create and call APIs from servers. While these are Web APIs in the sense that they are implemented on the Web, usually the term "Web API," when used in relation to JavaScript, refers to a special type of API. We have briefly covered Web APIs throughout the book, and we've discussed how they allow for a type of multithreading. How this works can be seen in Figure 11-1.

© Jonathon Simpson 2023
J. Simpson, *How JavaScript Works*, https://doi.org/10.1007/978-1-4842-9738-4_11

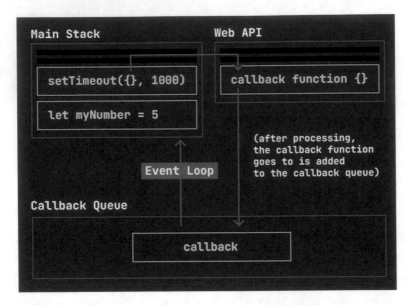

Figure 11-1. *Web APIs are processed separately from your main JavaScript stack. They usually interact with the operating system or run some more complicated code in the background (in languages like C, C++, or Rust). Web APIs abstract the complexity into a few function calls*

The diagram in Figure 11-1 gives you a hint at how Web APIs differ from APIs built on a server. Web APIs exist within your browser. They usually provide an interface between JavaScript and the operating system.

Just like other APIs, Web APIs abstract complexity away from the programmer. For example, the Web API we use for sending notifications to the user via their operating system's notification system may be simple to call in JavaScript, but under the hood, this API will run some more complicated code in other languages (like C and C++) to cause the operating system to display a notification to the user.

Every Web API exists on the window object. That means that while we could write window.fetch() to use the fetch API, it's much more common to omit window and simply run fetch().

The list of Web APIs is long, and new APIs are developed all the time. As well as that, support often varies from browser to browser for many of them. As such, we won't cover them all but instead focus on the ones you will find most useful for browser-based JavaScript development.

Web APIs usually arise from a specific need that is unfulfilled which many developers frequently require. For example, the Web Storage API is a Web API for storing data on a user's local computer. Many Web APIs do not have cross-browser support and are considered experimental, meaning you need to be careful when using them. Although Web Storage is broadly accepted these days, you may find developers checking if the browser supports them by checking if they exist on the window object. All Web APIs exist on the global window object, so you can check for this support as is shown have done in the following example:

```
if(window.localStorage) {
    // The browser supports local storage
}
```

Frequently Used Web APIs

Web APIs usually give us fundamental functionality that many developers find useful. Take notifications as an example. Historically, developers built notifications into the website as `<div>` elements that would appear upon some user action. This meant many thousands of notification implementations. JavaScript then came up with the Web Notification API to give us a standard way to notify users from our applications. This did two things:

- It improved the UX for users, giving them recognizable notifications instead of custom in-browser versions.

- It meant developers could spend more time solving other problems rather than building their own versions instead.

Here are four more examples of where JavaScript has improved developer experience through API:

- The URL API, used for parsing URLs

- The Web Storage API for managing storage locally

- The Notification API for sending notifications

- The History API

Let's look at these in detail to understand the problems they solve.

URL API

Before the *URL API*, developers would have to write their own scripts to parse a URL, and many times, these were poorly implemented. The URL API is a simple and standard Web API that can parse URLs. It is implemented via the URL constructor, which parses a URL and returns an object of its components:

```
let myUrl = new URL("https://some-website.com/page")
console.log(myUrl) // Console logs the URL as an object of
                        components.
console.log(myUrl.pathname) // returns "/page"
```

Web Storage API

Before the *Web Storage API*, developers would store local data in the majority of cases through cookies and, if needed, via back-end APIs. For simple applications, back-end storage was often an overkill, meaning applications could be more bloated than they needed to be.

The Web Storage API is a broad term covering two things: sessionStorage and localStorage. This API allows you to store data locally on your user's computer. This can be useful for storing things like settings. For example, if the user changes the theme of your website, you could store such a setting in their localStorage.

While localStorage persists on your computer, sessionStorage is deleted when the page is closed. The localStorage and sessionStorage for a web page can be found under the Application tab in your console, as shown in Figure 11-2.

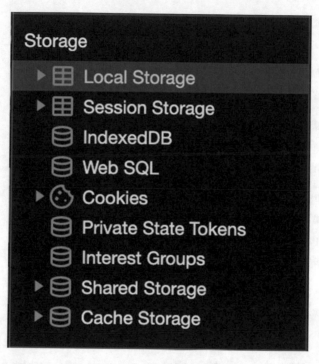

Figure 11-2. localStorage *and* sessionStorage *can be found along with other types of storage in the Application tab of your console in Chrome. Other browsers have similar summaries for you to view*

Using localStorage is much more common, but sessionStorage can find utility in some niche cases. Setting data in localStorage and sessionStorage works via the setItem method:

```
localStorage.setItem("someKey", "someValue")
sessionStorage.setItem("temporaryKey", "temporaryValue")
```

Both localStorage and sessionStorage store data in string format, so an object should be stringified with JSON.stringify() before being stored in your localStorage. Both localStorage and sessionStorage have the same methods:

- setItem(key, value) – To set a key–value pair in localStorage or sessionStorage.

- getItem(key) – To get the value of a key by the key's name, that is, localStorage.getKey("someKey").

- removeItem(key) – To remove a key–value pair by the key's name, that is, localStorage.removeItem("someKey").

- key(index) – To get the name of a key by the key's index, that is, key(0), to get the first key's name. In our example where someKey is the first key, then localStorage.key(0) will return "someKey".

- clear() – To clear all data in either the sessionStorage or localStorage, that is, localStorage.clear().

Note   The Web Storage API gives us a simple way to store data on a user's computer, but it is quite limited. As such, another storage API called the IndexedDB API exists to store more complex data. Complex data storage usually happens on the back end, so you may not find use for this, but it does exist if you have more complicated front-end storage needs.

Web Notifications API

The *Web Notification API* is not always used for notifications, but it gives developers a standard method for creating notifications from the browser. Notifications created this way are sent to the user via their operating system's built-in notification system. In a previous era, before we had access to this, we could only create notifications within the website's viewport itself.

The Notification API requires you to ask the user for permission to send notifications so that websites don't bother users with unnecessary messages. Requesting this access must come via a user gesture, such as clicking on a button:

```
document.getElementById("notification-button").
addEventListener(async (e) => {
    await Notification.requestPermission()
})
```

The user will then be asked to review this permission request, after which you can send them notifications. It's important to know that notifications can only be sent when the user has your web page open. Notifications also have some additional options, letting us set the title, body text, and icon for the notification:

```
const someNotification = new Notification("Some
Notification", {
  body: "Main body text",
  icon: "./images/some-image.png"
})
```

We can also close a particular notification by using the `.close()` method:

```
someNotification.close()
```

History API

Before the History API, it was basically impossible to manipulate a user's history from JavaScript. The History API lets us do this from the history global object. For example, we can force a user to navigate back and forward like so:

```
history.back() // Go back one page.
history.forward() // Go forward one page.
history.go(-2) // Go back two pages.
```

The History API also opens up the possibility of other functionality, such as letting us load a page without reloading. Before the History API, we could load a web page via API when a user clicked a link and then insert that page's contents into the user's <body> tag. Even though this was relatively easy to do, we had no way to let the user navigate back and forward with the browser's navigation buttons after doing this.

This creates an obvious and quite major UX problem! Fortunately, the History API solves this for us, allowing us to update the URL of the current page without the user having to reload.

To illustrate how this works, take a look at the following example. If we want to change the user's URL to have /page at the end, we can do this:

```
history.pushState({ "page" : "Some Page Title" }, "", "/page")
window.addEventListener("popstate", (event) => {
    console.log(event.state) // { "page" : "Some Page Title" }
})
```

For the user, the page will not reload, but the URL will change. The first parameter of pushState is data which is passed to the window's popstate event whenever pushState is fired. You can use this data to do something else to the page inside the popstate event listener. The second argument is never used and is usually left blank for historical reasons.

The last argument is the new page name of the URL. If you were on `https://google.com/` and fired this, the URL would change to `https://google.com/page`.

While `history.pushState()` creates a new entry in the user's history, you can also use `history.replaceState()` to replace the URL for the current entry in the user's history, too. This works in exactly the same way; only it won't create a new entry in the user's history, meaning pressing back will just go back to the previous page the user was on:

```
history.replaceState({ "page" : "Some Page Title" }, "", "/page")
```

Summary

The APIs we've covered previously all solve a specific need that JavaScript developers either had to create custom solutions for or simply couldn't do before. There are many more useful Web APIs, and here are a few more examples with more niche functionality, which have broad support in most modern browsers:

- The Performance Web API, used to monitor website performance (through `window.Performance`)

- The File System Web API, used to manipulate a user's local file system (through a variety of window methods, like `window.showOpenFilePicker()`)

- The Payments API, used to request payments via browser or OS built-in payment tools (think Apple or Google Pay) (through `window.PaymentRequest`)

- The Selection API, used to get the location of the caret when editing text or get a range of text characters currently selected by the user (through `window.Selection`)

When using Web APIs, it's important to check their browser support. Not all browsers support the same features in JavaScript, so some new Web APIs may work in Chrome, but not in Safari, for example. You can explore the full functionality of the preceding Web APIs and others in your own time or when your project needs them.

Functions, while loops, variables, and math are all fundamental to JavaScript, but it would be hard to do anything interactive on the Web without the use of Web APIs. Web APIs give us additional functionality on top of all the core tenets of JavaScript, like notifications, local storage, and HTTP requests. While we haven't covered every Web API here, the cool thing about JavaScript is that new ones are always being created. In the next couple chapters, we'll look at more Web APIs that provide further useful functionality to your JavaScript applications.

CHAPTER 12

Errors and the Console

Throughout this book, we've consistently relied on the console object to debug and learn more about how JavaScript works. We've also touched upon the fact that JavaScript can throw errors if you do something it doesn't understand. In this chapter, we'll dive deeper into how the console works, along with additional methods available to you so that you can get the most out of it. After we've fully explored the console, we'll look at errors and how to handle them.

The Console Object

The console object is one of the most useful objects available to you in JavaScript and we've used it extensively throughout this book.

If you are running Node.js, console logs appear in your terminal directly. For browsers, they appear in the developer tools, which can usually be accessed by right-clicking a web page and choosing **Inspect** or **Inspect Element**. All modern browsers have developer tools that include a console tab:

```
let x = 5
console.log(x) // console logs 5
```

© Jonathon Simpson 2023
J. Simpson, *How JavaScript Works*, https://doi.org/10.1007/978-1-4842-9738-4_12

The `console` object contains a multitude of other really useful methods for debugging. Let's dive into what these are, as you'll find that they come in handy when building larger applications.

Console Errors, Debugs, Warnings, and Info

As your code gets more complicated, you might find that you want to inform yourself or other developers via the console of major problems. For example, your API might not work if someone passes the wrong data to it, so you might want to return an error or a warning.

Console warnings and errors are accessed via `console.warning` and `console.error`, respectively. For example, if we wanted to create an error where the error text was "You did something bad!" we'd only need to do this:

```
console.error("You did something bad!")
```

As well as warnings and errors, we can invoke informative logs by using a method called `console.info` or debug messages using `console.debug`. Both work mostly the same as `console.log`. In some browsers, it will be `console.info` will be displayed as informative content, which means it may be formatted differently, while in all JavaScript implementations, `console.debug` will only be shown if debug messages are enabled by the user.

Console Tracing

If you have a long list of functions, you can trace the origin of them by using `console.trace`. This outputs what is known as a trace to the console. The resulting output of the following code can be seen in Figure 12-1.

```
function someFunction() {
    console.trace()
}

someFunction()
```

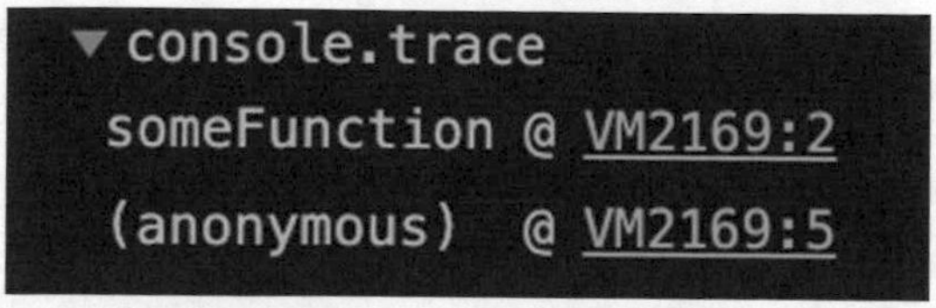

```
▼ console.trace
  someFunction @ VM2169:2
  (anonymous)  @ VM2169:5
```

Figure 12-1. *Console tracing can be useful when you have complicated functions. It tells you exactly which function called which and where in the code it's found*

Console Assertion

Another way to create errors with the console is `console.assert`. While related to console errors, `console.assert` is a little different in that it accepts multiple arguments, and it throws an error only if the first expression is false. The second argument is the error that will be shown to the user. In the following example, we assert that 5 is equal to 4. Since this is obviously false, an error with the error text, "the assertion is false," is shown to the user. This can be seen in Figure 12-2.

```
console.assert(5 === 4, "the assertion is false")
```

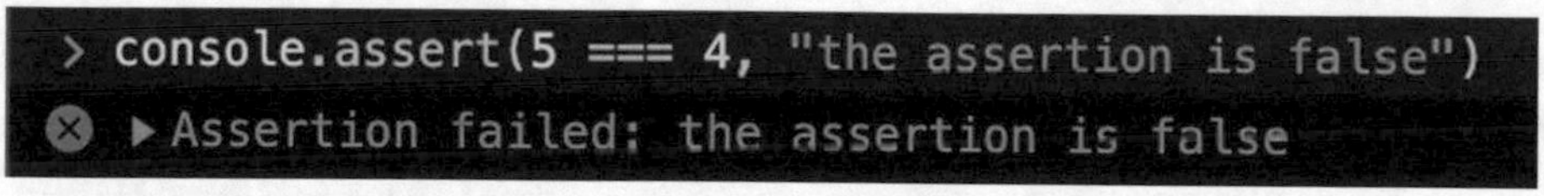

```
> console.assert(5 === 4, "the assertion is false")
⊗ ▸ Assertion failed: the assertion is false
```

Figure 12-2. *Console assertions let you show errors if certain criteria are found to be false*

Console Timing

Typical JavaScript code is not exactly known for its efficiency. If you write bad code in JavaScript, it has the propensity to take a really long time to process. For example, it's possible to write code that pauses execution via promises, waits for APIs to load, or has inefficient calculations that result in long wait times.

All of these impact page load time and therefore user experience. Search engines like Google use page load time to figure out where to place your website in search results. Therefore, optimizing your JavaScript is really important, and the best way to find code that is performing code is by measuring how long it takes to run. To help diagnose these problems, there are three console methods we can use. These are listed below:

- `console.time`

- `console.timeLog`

- `console.timeEnd`

Instead of console logging a specific string of text, these methods create timers, which return the time in milliseconds. If we wanted to create a timer with the name "my timer," we would first run `console.time("my timer")` to initiate the timer. From the point where that is called, the clock starts ticking.

Then when we want to log the time, we use `console.timeLog("my timer")` using the same name as we initiated with. When we want to stop, we use `console.timeEnd("my timer")`.

In the following example, we log three timers inside `setTimeout` functions:

```
console.time("my timer")

setTimeout(function() {
    console.timeLog("my timer")
}, 1000)

setTimeout(function() {
    console.timeLog("my timer")
    console.timeEnd("my timer")
}, 1500)
```

The output of this code in the console looks like this:

```
my timer: 1002.744140625 ms
my timer: 1506.8349609375 ms
my timer: 1507.031005859375 ms
```

As you can see, this is roughly correct, give or take a few milliseconds for processing the console method itself. You can call `console.timeLog` as many times as you want, and `console.timeEnd` will also result in one line of time recording in your console.

Console Counting

Another method that works the same as `console.time` is `console.count`. It accepts a unique value, and every time it is called, it will add 1 to the count for that value. For example:

```
console.count("my count")
console.count("my count")
console.count("my count")
```

This shows in the console as follows:

```
my count: 1
my count: 2
my count: 3
```

If you want to reset the counter to the beginning again, you can then use `console.countReset("my count")`.

Note   You can clear your console entirely by invoking `console.clear()`. This will work in browsers but will do nothing if your log is in a terminal (like when using Node.JS).

Other Useful Console Methods

If you want to find out the full power which console gives to you, just console log the console object to see all the methods at your disposal:

```
console.log(console)
```

We've covered many of the most useful console methods, and you can mess around with these in your own time. Let's look at the remaining methods and how they work in more detail.

Console Grouping

You can group console logs with `console.group` and `console.groupCollapsed`.

Both indent console logs, creating multiple levels of console. The main difference between both is that when using console.groupCollapsed, the groups are collapsed, and the user must expand them to read the console. In the following example, we create two levels of console log. The output of this can be seen in Figure 12-3.

```
console.log("Hi") // Top Level
console.group("Level 1") // Level 1 Group
console.log("Hi") // All of these are within Level 1 Group
console.log("Hi")
console.log("Hi")
console.group("Level 2") // Level 2 Group
console.log("Hi") // All of these are within Level 2 Group,
which are within Level 1
console.log("Hi")
```

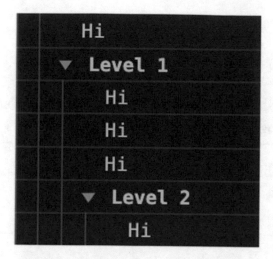

Figure 12-3. *A depiction of how console grouping looks. If using*
`console.groupCollapsed`, *the groups would be closed by default*
instead of expanded

Note   If you console an object using `console.dir` instead of
`console.log`, it creates an expandable view of the object like
shown when using `console.group`. This can be useful for deep
objects, where you only want to expand certain sections.

Console Tables

Finally, `console.table` allows you to create tables of objects or arrays. For
example, given the following input, we can produce a table as is shown in
Table 12-1.

```
const favoriteFruits = [
  ["Person", "Favorite Fruit"],
  ["John", "Apple"],
```

```
  ["Mary", "Raspberry"]
]
console.table(favoriteFruits)
```

Table 12-1. *Console.table gives us the ability to create table views inside the console*

Person	Favorite Fruit
John	Apple
Mary	Raspberry

The same method can be applied to objects. For example, the following code will create a table in the console similar to the one shown in Table 12-2.

```
const favoriteFruits = {
    "name" : "John",
    "age" : 105,
    "place" : "Planet Earth"
}
console.table(favoriteFruits)
```

Table 12-2. *Console.table supports both objects and arrays*

index	value
name	John
age	105
place	Planet Earth

Errors and Exceptions

We've now covered consoles and everything you can do with them. We've shown how you can create your own error messages using consoles too. In previous chapters, we've run into errors, which is when JavaScript runs into a problem that it cannot resolve. JavaScript is quite good at resolving most coding mistakes, so errors really are the last resort!

You'll run into all sorts of errors in JavaScript. The main kinds of errors in JavaScript are listed below:

- ReferenceError – We tried to reference a variable that did not exist.

- EvalError – An issue happened while we tried to run eval().

- TypeError – An issue happened due to something relating to type – that is, a function was expecting one type and got another.

- RangeError – An issue happened as we tried to call something outside the range of what was expected, that is, we called an array element that did not exist.

- AggregateError – An error which contains many errors.

- URIError – We have an invalid URI string or have used a URI function incorrectly.

We can avoid most errors or exceptions by ensuring our code is good quality and being strict about type control. In general, you'll want to avoid errors, but if you do run into them, there are ways to get around them too.

Note   Each of the preceding error types are standalone objects. That means `console.log(ReferenceError)` is valid JavaScript, for example.

---

try...catch

When we generate errors in our code, usually they terminate execution. That means JavaScript stops trying to process anything else. We obviously don't want that to happen, since it will break the user experience!

Sometimes though, errors can be unavoidable. For example, passing non-JSON values to `JSON.parse()` will usually result in an error. This can happen quite easily, especially if you are working with badly written APIs.

To prevent these kinds of errors from breaking our code, we can use `try...catch`:

```
try {
    let JSONData = JSON.parse(inputData)
}
catch (e) {
    console.log("Could not parse JSON!")
    let JSONData = {}
}
```

If the code passes with no errors, then great – we have parsed some JSON. If it does not, then the error is "caught" in the `catch` statement. The e in `catch` refers to the error text itself with a trace of where the error came from.

Using a catch statement here gives us the opportunity to not only prevent an error from causing our code to stop execution but also to set the JSONData variable to an empty object, in case we need to reference JSONData later.

We can generate our own errors on purpose using the throw control statement. Usually we use this when something bad has happened in our code, and we want to end execution. When used in a try...catch block, it results in the catch block always being used:

```
try {
    throw "Some Error"
}
catch (e) {
    console.log("An error was generated")
}
```

finally

We can supplement try...catch with a finally statement, which will immediately fire before a control statement from a try or catch block or before execution completes where a control statement does not exist.

A finally statement does not catch the error. That means if you omit the catch, an error will still be thrown. In the following example, finally will run before the error appears since finally runs immediately before any control statements (think return, throw, break or continue) complete. That means JSONData is defined as {} in the following example even though an error is still thrown (since "ok" is not valid JSON):

```
try {
    let JSONData = JSON.parse("ok")
}
finally {
    let JSONData = {}
}
```

If we had caught this error, then JSONData would have been set to {}, and the error would not have been shown at all. This allows us to separate out the catching of the error from defining alternatives:

```
try {
    let JSONData = JSON.parse("ok")
}
catch(e) {
    console.log("Your JSON is invalid")
}
finally {
    let JSONData = {}
    console.log(JSONData)
}
```

Since finally will run control statements before try and catch complete, it can be used to mask the value of try and catch control statements. For example, in the following example we try to return some valid JSON. This is returned, but finally always fires before the last control statement in a try or catch. As such, the return value is set to {} since that is what finally returns. A diagram of the try...catch...finally flow can be found in Figure 12-4.

```
function someFunction() {
    try {
        return { "hello" : "world" }
    }
    finally {
        return {}
    }
}

console.log(someFunction()) // Console logs {}
```

Note   We've covered control statements before, just under different topics. Control statements can be `break`, `throw`, `return`, or `continue`.

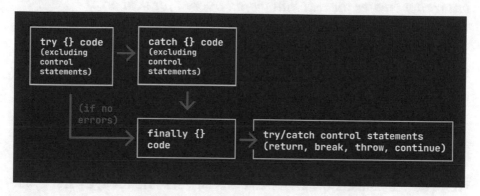

Figure 12-4. *Finally will always fire before try and catch control statements. However, the rest of the try and catch code before the control statement will be executed before finally*

Generating Errors

We have already seen how `throw` can be used to generate errors. Errors generated with throw stop code execution, unless caught in a `try...catch` statement.

We can get more control over our error statements by using the new `Error()` constructor instead. However, by itself, `new Error()` does not actually generate a new error as the code suggests! Instead, it creates the text that would appear in the error. In the following example, the error generated will not stop execution but generate a text string with the line on which `new Error()` was generated from. You can see what that looks like in Figure 12-5.

```
new Error("Hello World")
```

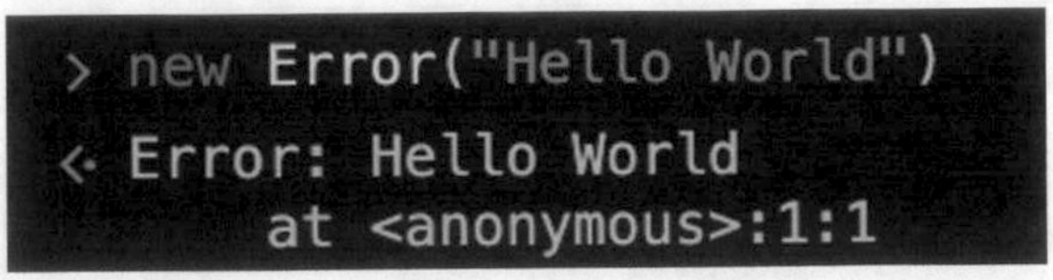

```
> new Error("Hello World")
< Error: Hello World
      at <anonymous>:1:1
```

Figure 12-5. *Using the* `Error` *constructor does not create a new error but rather creates the text that would appear for that error*

If you want to generate an execution breaking error, you have to throw your error, too:

```
throw new Error("Hello World")
```

Handling Specific Errors

We've now looked at how to generate errors, but sometimes, a part of your code can be known to have the potential to throw multiple types of errors. Separating these errors out to handle each individually can be useful. We can check for error types using the `instanceof` keyword and then handle specific error cases in different ways. In the following example, we create two error handling routes: one if the error is a `SyntaxError` and another if it is an `EvalError`:

```
try {
    JSON.parse("OK")
} catch(e) {
    if(e instanceof SyntaxError) {
        console.log("This is a syntax error");
    } else if(e instanceof EvalError) {
        console.log("This was an error with the eval()
        function");
    }
}
```

In this example, since `JSON.parse("OK")` is a `SyntaxError`, the first console log will fire.

Summary

In this chapter, we've covered all the key principles around JavaScript consoles. We've shown you that there are many useful methods found on the console object, which can be used to bring more meaning to your console logs.

We've also discussed errors. We've covered all the types of errors that JavaScript can throw at you and how to catch errors through `try... catch...finally` statements. Finally, we've shown how you can generate your own errors using throw statements.

Error management and console logging are really important in ensuring your users have a good experience. Ideally, users should not be exposed to raw errors, and developers should have access to good console logs. By becoming familiar with everything we've covered here, you can begin to add these best practice principles into your code.

CHAPTER 13

The Canvas

So far, we have only dealt with code that is used either directly in JavaScript or on the HTML DOM. Operations to modify the DOM are easy to do in JavaScript, but they are relatively slow when compared to other JavaScript code. You'll begin to notice these inefficiencies if you have thousands of DOM elements on your page and apply interactions to them using addEventListener. This makes creating DOM-based games or large interactive applications like whiteboards nearly impossible from a performance perspective. At one point, I learned this the hard way when trying to recreate the original Mario game by using a one HTML DOM element to a one-pixel scale. Eventually, such complex applications become totally unresponsive.

Some JavaScript frameworks try to improve on DOM inefficiencies by converting the entire DOM into an object, called the Virtual DOM. This is useful for websites wanting to load faster but still does not address the former problem, where just having many DOM elements becomes problematic in large applications.

To get around this problem, and others, we have an HTML element called <canvas> and an associated JavaScript Canvas API, which lets us draw interactive content onto a single HTML element. Canvas is just normal JavaScript code, with a few additional functions and methods that allow us to draw. It is much more efficient than large scale DOM–based applications but is not really recommended as a way to build entire websites in. Instead, canvas should be used for small pieces of interactive content, interactive games, or parts of interactive applications. In this chapter, we'll cover how the Canvas API works in JavaScript.

© Jonathon Simpson 2023
J. Simpson, *How JavaScript Works*, https://doi.org/10.1007/978-1-4842-9738-4_13

Introduction

To get started with HTML canvas, we first need to create a <canvas> element. This empty tag becomes the container for the graphic we will produce via JavaScript. In HTML, we can create a canvas by writing the following code:

```
<canvas id="canvasElement" width="500" height="400"></canvas>
```

You may see canvas with predefined width and height, which is useful if the graphic we're producing has to have a certain size. You could set your canvas to be of width and height 100%, too.

Once set up, we can reference our canvas in JavaScript using any JavaScript selector method:

```
let myCanvas = document.getElementById("canvasElement")

// Set the context of our canvas
let context = myCanvas.getContext("2d")
```

When we use getContext on a <canvas> element, like we have in the preceding context variable, it generates a new object with all of the additional methods required to work with canvas. You can console log context itself to see these methods:

```
console.log(context)
```

By using these methods, we can draw directly onto the canvas HTML element.

The preceding object created is a CanvasRenderingContext2D object since the context we used is 2D. That means the expectation is we will only create 2D drawings on our canvas. Additional contexts can be applied. The full list is shown in the following:

- `canvas.getContext("2d")` – Creates a `CanvasRenderingContext2D` object for 2D drawing.

- `canvas.getContext("webgl")` – Creates a `WebGLRenderingContext` object. This is only available if your browser supports webGL but gives additional methods for working in a 3D space.

- `canvas.getContext("webgpu")` – Creates a `GPUCanvasContext` object. This is only available if your browser supports webGPU – the successor to webGL.

- `canvas.getContext("bitmaprenderer")` – Creates an `ImageBitmapRenderingContext` object. This is used for drawing images onto the canvas. ImageBitmaps are more performant than other image data since they are processed directly on the GPU.

All of these settings create objects with useful methods in each context. In this chapter, we will focus on the 2d context as it is the most widely used. From here on out, most of the work on our canvas element stems from the context variable.

Reminder   When referencing the canvas element as we have done earlier, make sure you place your JavaScript at the end of your file – otherwise, the canvas element will return null. Alternatively, you can add the `DOMContentLoaded` event to your document and place your canvas code within that event listener. We covered this in Chapter 8.

Drawing and Images

Drawing shapes on a canvas requires using methods available on the context variable created with getContext("2d"). WebGL, Bitmap, and WebGPU contexts will have different methods, so ensure you have the right context set up.

Drawing Rectangles

Three main methods exist for drawing rectangles:

- context.rect(x, y, width, height) – Outlines where a rectangle or square should be but does not fill it.

- context.fillRect(x, y, width, height) – Creates a rectangle and immediately fills it.

- context.strokeRect(x, y, width, height) – Creates a rectangle and immediately outlines it with a stroke.

For each of these the arguments x, y, width, and height refer to a pixel coordinate to draw the rectangle. Therefore the width and height of your canvas become quite important. The width and height you set on your canvas element is the drawing location.

For example, if your canvas was 400px by 600px in size, drawing something at point 500px, 700px would be not visible, as it would no longer be on the canvas – however, drawing something at 200px, 200px would be 200px in on both the x and y coordinates.

Note   If you change the size of your canvas with CSS, it will not affect the drawing area; that can only be affected by the width and height properties. That means that if the canvas HTML element is 200px by 200px, and you set width and height to 100px by 100px, the resolution of the canvas will double!

By themselves, the rectangle functions are not of much use. You need to combine them with other methods for them to become visible. For example, if we want to create a rectangle, `context.rect()` will create the "information" about where the rectangle is, but `context.fill()` and `context.stroke()` are required to give it a color and outline, respectively:

```
let canvas = document.getElementById("canvasElement")
let context = canvas.getContext("2d")

context.rect(10, 10, 100, 150)
context.fill()
context.stroke()
```

By default, the stroke and fill color are both black. We can further enhance our drawings by setting custom stroke widths, fill colors, and stroke colors by using `lineWidth`, `fillStyle`, and `stokeStyle`, respectively:

```
let canvas = document.getElementById("canvasElement")
let context = canvas.getContext("2d")

context.rect(10, 10, 100, 150)
context.fillStyle = "#8effe0"
context.strokeStyle = "#42947e"
context.lineWidth = 5
context.fill()
context.stroke()
```

It's worth noting that canvas in HTML is sequentially written. The fill style will apply to any drawn elements until another is drawn. So if we wanted to draw two rectangles beside each other in different colors, we'd have to update the values of `fillStyle` and `strokeStyle`. We also have to start each new shape with the `beginPath` method. That way, canvas will know that the fill and stroke styles apply only to specific rectangles. You can see an example of that code in the following and an illustration of what it will look like in Figure 13-1.

```
context.beginPath()
context.rect(10, 10, 100, 150)
context.fillStyle = "#8effe0"
context.strokeStyle = "#42947e"
context.lineWidth = 5
context.fill()
context.stroke()
context.closePath()
context.beginPath()
context.rect(120, 10, 100, 150)
context.fillStyle = "#42947e"
context.strokeStyle = "#8effe0"
context.lineWidth = 5
context.fill()
context.stroke()
```

Figure 13-1. *Two rectangles draw beside each other in separate colors using beginPath*

Both context.strokeRect and context.fillRect work the same way as context.rect; only there is no need to call context.stroke() and context.fill(), respectively.

Drawing Circles

Two methods exist on 2d canvas contexts to draw circles:

- `context.arc()` for drawing regular arcs

- `context.ellipse()` for drawing ellipses rather than circles

The `arc()` method has the following arguments, with the last being optional:

`ctx.arc(x, y, radius, startAngle, endAngle, counterClockwise?)`

Each of these arguments can be found below:

- `x` – Refers to the x coordinate of the center of the circle

- `y` – Refers to the y coordinate of the center of the circle

- `radius` – The radius of the arc we are drawing

- `startAngle` – The angle at which the arc starts (in radians)

- `endAngle` – The angle at which the arc ends (in radians)

- `counterClockwise` – Whether the angle goes counterclockwise (default is false, can be set to true)

Meanwhile, the `ellipse()` method has the following arguments:

`ctx.ellipse(x, y, radiusX, radiusY, rotation, startAngle, endAngle, counterClockwise?)`

The arguments here are similar. Here is the full list along with definitions:

- `x` – Refers to the x coordinate of the center of the circle

- `y` – Refers to the y coordinate of the center of the circle

- radiusX – The radius along the x axis of the arc we are drawing

- radiusY – The radius along the y axis of the arc we are drawing

- rotation – How much we wish to rotate our ellipse shape, in radians

- startAngle – The angle at which the arc starts (in radians)

- endAngle – The angle at which the arc ends (in radians)

- counterClockwise – Whether the angle goes counterclockwise (default is false, can be set to true)

Since both use radians for degrees, we have to use the Math.PI constants to refer to angles for each. In the following example, we create a full circle using context.arc(), since 2π is equal to 360 degrees:

```
let canvas = document.getElementById("canvasElement")
let context = canvas.getContext("2d")

context.arc(100, 100, 45, 0, Math.PI * 2, false)
context.fillStyle = "#42947e"
context.fill()
```

You can create semicircles too by using Math.PI instead of Math. PI * 2. You can also begin your circle at any starting angle, too. Here is an example of a pie chart, created by drawing only a sideways semicircle beside our original circle:

```
// Semi Circle (Math.PI * 1 is a semi circle)
context.beginPath()
context.arc(210, 100, 45, Math.PI * 1.5, Math.PI * 2.5, false)
context.fill()
```

When creating ellipses, two radii are used: radiusX and radiusY allow us to squish or morph a circle along two axes. Let's add an ellipse to our group, too. You can see all three of our circles in Figure 13-2.

```
context.beginPath()
context.ellipse(350, 100, 45, 25, 0, Math.PI * 2, false)
context.fillStyle = "#42947e"
context.fill()
```

Figure 13-2. *Our final group of circles – one created using* Math.PI ** 2 radians, the second* Math.PI *radians, and the final one using two radii via the* ellipse() *method*

Note   After drawing on a canvas, you can clear a section of it or your entire canvas by calling canvas.clearRect(x, y, width, height). This will clear a portion of the canvas starting at the x and y coordinates and ending at the width and height.

Drawing Triangles

Since there are no triangle methods in canvas, we have to make our own. To do that, we need to learn about the moveTo and lineTo methods. The first moves the starting point of a line to a specific position, and the second draws a line between that point and another. Creating an equilateral triangle looks like this:

```
let canvas = document.getElementById("canvasElement")
let context = canvas.getContext("2d")

context.moveTo(20, 0)
context.lineTo(40, 30)
context.lineTo(0, 30)
context.lineTo(20, 0)
context.fillStyle = "#42947e"
context.fill()
```

Since moveTo does not draw lines, we can draw multiple triangles (or indeed, as many different types of shapes as we want using moveTo and lineTo. In the following, we draw two identical triangles using this method. You can also see this code in action in Figure 13-3.

```
context.moveTo(20, 0)
context.lineTo(40, 30)
context.lineTo(0, 30)
context.lineTo(20, 0)

context.moveTo(80, 0)
context.lineTo(100, 30)
context.lineTo(60, 30)
context.lineTo(80, 0)
context.fillStyle = "#b668ff"
context.fill()
```

Figure 13-3. *Two identical triangles drawn using the moveTo and lineTo methods*

Drawing Images

While drawing shapes is useful when working with the canvas, you may also find yourself needing to add images. Images work a little differently from what we've seen so far. To create a new image, we have to use the image constructor to add them to our canvas.

Since images are loaded over HTTP, we also need to wait for them to load before we can add them to our canvas. Here is an example of how we do that:

```
// Create our image
let newImage = new Image()
newImage.src = "https://google.com/some-image.png"

// When it loads
newImage.onload = () => {
    // Draw the image onto the context
    context.drawImage(newImage, 0, 0, 250, 208);
}
```

`context.drawImage()` is the method used to draw the image onto our canvas. It is similar to previous methods, where it takes x and y coordinates, along with the width and height you wish the image to be displayed at:

```
context.drawImage(image, x, y, width, height)
```

A more complicated version of this method is also available, which allows for cropping:

```
ctx.drawImage(image, cx, cy, sw, sh, x, y, width, height)
```

The definitions for each argument in this version are shown in the following list. You can also see a demonstration of how these arguments alter the image in Figure 13-4.

- `image` – The image we want to use, generated from our `new Image()` constructor.

- `cx` – This is how far from the top left we want to crop the image by. So if it is 50, the image will be cropped 50px from the left-hand side.

- `cy` – This is how far from the top we want to crop the image by. So if it is 50, the image will be cropped 50px from the top side.

- `sw` – This is how big we want the image to be from the point of cx. So if 100, the image will continue for 100px from cx and then be cropped at that point.

- `sh` – This is how big we want the image to be from the point of ch. So if 100, the image will continue for 100px from ch and then be cropped at that point.

- `x` – The x position on the canvas for the top left corner of the image.

- `y` – The y position on the canvas for the top left corner of the image.

- `width` – The width of the image. If left blank, the original image width is used.

- `height` – The height of the image. If left blank, the original image height is used.

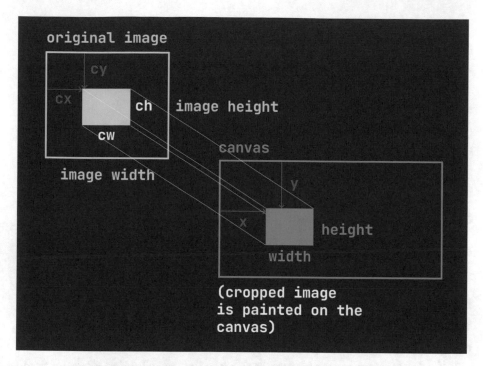

Figure 13-4. *An example of how image cropping works. The image is first cropped using the arguments* cx, cy, cw, *and* ch. *That cropped image is then painted on the canvas at positions* x *and* y, *with a width of* width *and* height

Drawing Text

Now that we've covered images and shapes, let's take a look at how we can add text to a canvas. As with previous examples, various functions and properties also exist to add text to a canvas:

```
let canvas = document.getElementById("canvasElement")
let context = canvas.getContext("2d")

context.font = "bold 88px Arial"
context.strokeStyle = "red"
context.lineWidth = 4
context.strokeText("Hello World!", 100, 200)
```

The preceding example will create text with a 4px red stroke, at position 100x200px. We can also use `fillText()`, if we want to fill the text with a specific color instead. Using either does not prevent us from using `fillStyle` with `fill()` or `strokeStyle` with `stroke()`, so you can decide which method to use based on what is more useful.

It's worth noting that by default, the 100x200px is taken from the bottom left of the text, at the text's baseline, rather than the top left. To change where the y coordinate is drawn from, we can change the text's baseline. For example, the following code will draw the y coordinate from the middle of the text instead:

```
context.textBaseline = "middle"
```

Any normal text baseline is accepted. You will be familiar with these if you've ever used text baselines in CSS. The accepted values are `top`, `middle`, `bottom`, `hanging`, `alphabetic`, and `ideographic`, where ideographic only really applies to East Asian scripts.

Similarly, we can change where the x coordinate begins drawing from by using `textAlign`, which can be set to left to start drawing from the `left` of the text, `center` to start drawing from the middle, and `right` to start drawing from the far right:

```
context.textAlign = "center"
```

Note   You will need to change the `textBaseline` or `textAlign` before stroking the text; otherwise it the change will not be rendered

---

The methods we've covered so far for drawing rectangles, circles, triangles/lines, images, and text are only the beginning. You can find all methods available to you by console logging the context variable. Try playing around to see what you can do!

Interactivity and Creating a Drawing Application

To practice what we've learned so far, let's create a simple drawing application, which will allow the user to draw directly onto the canvas. Since the canvas is an HTML DOM element like any other, it is also susceptible to the same methods as any other HTML DOM element. However, since the canvas does not contain elements itself, any events need to be added to the canvas alone, which means you often have to do a bit more mathematics to find out what the user is doing. Consider our use case's basic requirements:

- We have a canvas element.

- When a user clicks the element and drags, we want to track their mouse position and draw a line as they drag.

- When they let go, the line will no longer be drawn.

- The user can then draw more lines if they want to.

This sounds complicated, but it consists of only three events:

- An event for when the user clicks the canvas to initiate dragging (`pointerdown`)

- An event for when the user drags (`pointermove`) to draw the line

- An event for when the user lets go (`pointerup`) to stop the rectangle from being dragged anymore

For this example, we'll be using the following HTML canvas element:

```
<canvas id="canvasElement" width="500" height="400"></canvas>
```

In code, the three events we just described can be defined as shown in the following code. We can use a variable called `clicked` to store the state of whether a user clicked or not. If they click, `clicked` becomes true, and therefore dragging is occurring. If they let go, then clicked is false, and dragging has stopped. While clicked is true, we can track the user's cursor position and draw a rectangle in the right place:

```
let clicked
canvas.addEventListener("pointerdown", (e) => {
    clicked = true
})

canvas.addEventListener("pointermove", (e) => {
    if(clicked) {
        // Dragging is occurring
    }
})

canvas.addEventListener("pointerup", (e) => {
    clicked = false
})
```

Since the down and up events only control when drawing starts and stops, let's focus in on pointermove, where most of the logic for drawing will sit. There are two things to consider here:

- We can use e.pageX and e.pageY to get the live position of the user's cursor relative to the page.

- The canvas itself exists on a web page, and as such it is not necessarily at the top left of the page. We therefore have to calculate the user's cursor relative to the canvas.

Therefore, we need to get the canvas' top left position and subtract this from the cursor position in order to calculate where the user is clicking inside the canvas. An image demonstrating how this works can be found in Figure 13-5.

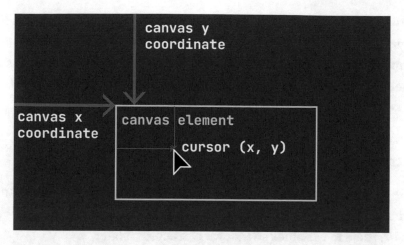

Figure 13-5. *Getting a cursor's position within an element can be achieved by subtracting the element's position from the cursor's position. That way, when the cursor is at the top left of the element, it is add (0, 0). Previously, canvas x and y coordinates can be retrieved via* canvas.getBoundingClientRect()'s *x and y properties. The cursor x and y can be retrieved by* e.pageX *and* e.pageY, *respectively*

To get the canvas position, we use an HTML DOM method called getBoundingClientRect(). We covered this function in a previous chapter, but getBoundingClientRect() gives us all the location data on a particular HTML element, as is shown below:

- x – The x position of the element's top left corner

- y – The y position of the element's top left corner

- width – The width of the element

- height – The height of the element

- top – The position of the top of the element

- left – The position of the left of the element

- right – The position of the right of the element

- bottom – The position of the bottom of the element

All of these properties include padding and border width, but not margin. So x refers to where the border starts, and not the margin, for example. We can access these on our canvas element by selecting the canvas element, and then applying the appropriate getBoundingClientRect() method. For example, we can get the x coordinate like so:

```
let canvas = document.getElementById("canvasElement")
let canvasXPosition = canvas.getBoundingClientRect().x
```

As we just described, we can get the cursor position relative to the canvas by subtracting the canvas position from the cursor position. We will store this data in variables so that we can access it later.

```
canvas.addEventListener("pointermove", (e) => {
    if(clicked) {
        let canvasPosition = canvas.getBoundingClientRect()
        let cursorLeft = e.pageX - canvasPosition.x
        let cursorTop = e.pageY - canvasPosition.y
        console.log(cursorLeft, cursorTop)
    }
})
```

The final step in our canvas interactivity use case is to draw a line as the user moves their "pressed down" cursor. To simplify this, I've decided to just draw a 5x5px rectangle every time the user drags their cursor. Our final code lets us draw on the canvas element, as expected in the original requirements.

```
let canvas = document.getElementById("canvasElement")
let context = canvas.getContext("2d")

let clicked

canvas.addEventListener("pointerdown", (e) => {
    clicked = true
})
```

```
canvas.addEventListener("pointermove", (e) => {
    if(clicked) {
          let canvasPosition = canvas.getBoundingClientRect()
        let cursorLeft = e.pageX - canvasPosition.x
        let cursorTop = e.pageY - canvasPosition.y

    context.rect(cursorLeft, cursorTop, 5, 5)
    context.fill()

  }
})

canvas.addEventListener("pointerup", (e) => {
    clicked = false
})
```

Animations

The final piece of functionality that the Canvas API can help us with is smooth animations. To perform animations in general, we usually use the top-level requestAnimationFrame() method. This is actually a pretty cool function, which calls any function passed to it 60 times per second, producing an effective frame rate of 60fps.

The function passed to requestAnimationFrame gains an argument, usually referred to as timestamp, which is the current timestamp in milliseconds for the request. Since requestAnimationFrame calls 60 times per second, you won't get a result for every millisecond!

In the following example, we use requestAnimationFrame to create a recursive function. A recursive function is simply one that calls itself again and again, which means the function can be called continuously on a 60fps cycle. For this animation, we'll be using this HTML canvas tag:

```
<canvas id="canvasElement" width="500" height="400"></canvas>
```

Since this would just last forever, we limit this recursion until the timeStamp is more than 50000 milliseconds – or 50 seconds. That will result in an animation which is 50 seconds long. This way, we don't end up with a function that runs until infinity.

The following animation creates a rectangle every 10 pixels, giving the illusion of a box that is filling up with 10x10px rectangles. While this is quite a simple animation, you can imagine how this could be changed to make more complicated computations. You can see how this animation looks part way through in Figure 13-6.

```
let canvas = document.getElementById("canvasElement")
let context = canvas.getContext("2d")

let y = 0
let x = -500
function drawCanvas(timeStamp) {
    x += 10
    let xCoordinate = x + 490
    if(x > 0) {
        x = -500
        y += 10
    }
    context.rect(xCoordinate, y, 10, 10)
    context.fill()
    // If timestamp is less than 50s, then run the animation
    // keyframe
    if(timeStamp < 50000) {
        requestAnimationFrame(drawCanvas)
    }
}

requestAnimationFrame(drawCanvas)
```

Figure 13-6. *The canvas is the perfect place to perform animations since we aren't burdened by slow DOM updates. By using* `requestAnimationFrame()`, *we can also ensure a smooth 60fps animation*

Summary

In this chapter, we've covered everything you need to get started with HTML canvas. You should know enough from this chapter to play around with it yourself. We've discussed how you can draw shapes, add text or images, and then subsequently add interactivity to your canvas via event listeners. We've also covered animations, which can be used to create interactive experiences for users in the browser.

The Canvas API is an efficient way to draw content for users or add interactivity to certain views. It also supports 3D contexts too, which can be utilized to create games in the browser. We won't cover here how 3D contexts work, but a popular framework called Three.JS can help you get started with that.

CHAPTER 14

Web Workers and Multithreading

Most implementations of JavaScript are single-threaded, with some exceptions. As JavaScript has begun to do more and more in terms of computation, the fact that a lot of processing is confined to a single thread has become somewhat limiting even with Web APIs to bear some of that load. On a single thread, for example, poorly written but computationally intensive code can stop the entire application from working.

To solve this problem and many more, the Web Workers API has been designed to give JavaScript a generic way to implement multiple threads, allowing complicated applications to outsource certain functionality to other threads on the same device. In this chapter, we'll be exploring what web workers are and how they work in both Node.JS and on the front end.

Introduction

Web workers are an advanced concept, and they are not needed for everyday JavaScript. If you are creating a website, you probably don't need web workers. In fact, you won't *need* web workers to do anything in JavaScript – but you'll probably want them for some things.

An example of where web workers become useful is when you have written something that requires heavy computation. For example, imagine you have an advanced image processor. If the image processor takes

© Jonathon Simpson 2023
J. Simpson, *How JavaScript Works*, https://doi.org/10.1007/978-1-4842-9738-4_14

five minutes to run, your single-threaded JavaScript will be frozen until that operation is completed. With web workers, you can outsource that processing to another thread, so that it doesn't take up your main thread.

Note   You cannot run a web worker in JS files on your computer. It needs to be run on a server. That means you can set up your own Node.JS server as we did in Chapter 10, or you can get a web host to host your files on.

In Chapter 5, we discussed how JavaScript can outsource calculations to Web APIs, which process code on a separate thread, and then pass it back to JavaScript via the event loop. Web workers work in a similar way, as shown in Figure 14-1.

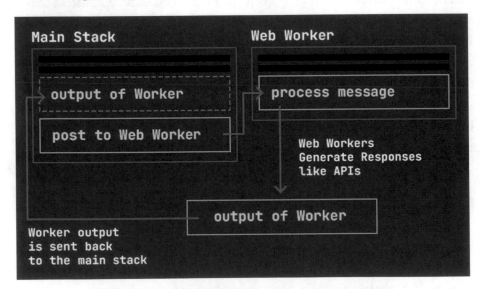

Figure 14-1. *Messages can be sent to web workers, causing the web worker to start processing. Then, an output will be produced, which can be captured on the main stack by events, for processing by the main thread*

Since web workers still result in code coming back to the stack, you may need to think about how you outsource computation. For example, an API running via fetch still has its own thread on the server and does computation asynchronously without affecting your front-end JavaScript code. Therefore, an API may be all you need to fulfill your needs. Web workers are most useful when you want to create multithreaded code locally, without relying on API servers.

Using Web Workers

In the browser and on the front end, web workers start out with the new Worker() constructor. For example, we can set the file some-worker.js to be a web worker by running the following code:

```
const myWorker = new Worker("./thread.js")
```

Web worker files are in a special format, and in the browser, they consist of a single onmessage event. Inside that, there is usually a postMessage function, which contains the data we want to send back to the main thread. For example, a simple web worker file, like thread.js, might look like this:

```
onmessage = function(c) {
    postMessage(`Worker Data: ${e.data}`)
}
```

Sending Messages to and from Web Workers

In thread.js, the onmessage event is what happens any time the worker receives input. The postMessage function is what is sent back to the main thread:

```
onmessage = function(e) {
    postMessage(`Worker Data: ${e.data}`)
}
```

In our main JavaScript file, we can send data to our worker by using postMessage on the worker:

```
const myWorker = new Worker("./thread.js")
myWorker.postMessage("Hello World")
```

The worker data is received by the worker, and it is stored in e.data. We can do whatever we want with this data – for example, if we sent an object like this:

```
const myWorker = new Worker("./thread.js")
myWorker.postMessage({ startScript: true })
```

Oftentimes, you'll find code triggering web workers on some kind of user-based event, like clicking a button:

```
document.getElementById('button').addEventListener('click',
function(e) {
    myWebWorker.postMessage({ "message" : "outcome" });
});
```

We could use a message from a user event in the thread.js file to trigger some kind of processing. When the processing is done, we can send a message back to the main thread. This can be any type of data, such as an object or string. In our hypothetical example where our web worker is an image processor, postMessage could send back a processed image to the main thread:

```
onmessage = function(e) {
    if(e.data.startScript === true) {
        // .. Do something
```

```
    postMessage({"processing" : "done"})
  }
}
```

When the worker sends data back to the main thread, we can capture the data using the onmessage method attached to the worker constructor:

```
const myWorker = new Worker("./thread.js")
myWorker.postMessage("Hello World")

myWorker.onmessage = (e) => {
    console.log(e.data)
}
```

Note   Web workers can use fetch() just like regular JavaScript code. That means you can outsource expensive APIs to web workers where necessary.

Web workers also have an onerror method, for capturing any errors that occur inside your web worker:

```
const myWorker = new Worker("./thread.js")
myWorker.postMessage("Hello World")

myWorker.onerror = (err, file, line) => {
    console.log(`${err} occurred in ${file} on line ${line}`)
}
```

Restrictions on Web Workers

While web workers give us a useful way to outsource some heavy computation to a separate thread, they do have some limitations. The three big limitations on Web Workers are as follows:

- As mentioned at the start of the chapter, you cannot run a web worker from your computer. It needs to be run on a server.

- Web workers cannot directly access and update the DOM.

- They only have limited access to globalThis or window properties. For example, they have no access to `localStorage`, but they do have access to `setTimeout`. You can find out all the APIs and window properties available by console logging `globalThis` in the worker itself.

Since web workers have some restrictions on the types of methods that can be called, it can be useful to console log the globalThis property inside your web worker thread. You can also find this information online, via websites like developer.mozilla.org:

```
console.log(globalThis)
```

You can see the different methods available to you in web workers by console logging `globalThis`. The outcome can be seen in Figure 14-2.

```
▼ DedicatedWorkerGlobalScope {name: '', onmes
  ▶ cancelAnimationFrame: ƒ cancelAnimationFra
  ▶ close: ƒ close()
    name: ""
  ▶ onmessage: ƒ (e)
    onmessageerror: null
  ▶ postMessage: ƒ postMessage()
  ▶ requestAnimationFrame: ƒ requestAnimation
  ▶ webkitRequestFileSystem: ƒ webkitRequestF
  ▶ webkitRequestFileSystemSync: ƒ webkitRequ
  ▶ webkitResolveLocalFileSystemSyncURL: ƒ we
  ▶ webkitResolveLocalFileSystemURL: ƒ webkit
    Infinity: Infinity
  ▶ AbortController: ƒ AbortController()
  ▶ AbortSignal: ƒ AbortSignal()
  ▶ AggregateError: ƒ AggregateError()
  ▶ Array: ƒ Array()
```

Figure 14-2. *Web workers have their own dedicated* globalThis, *which is different from window. You can test it out yourself by using* console.log(globalThis)

Conclusion

Web workers are a useful way to create multiple threads in your JavaScript code. While Web APIs and servers also give you ways to create multiple threads, web workers are a dedicated feature that allows you to create multiple threads independently.

JavaScript is quite performant because of the event loop and stacks. Therefore, web workers are only really useful for the most intensive computation functions. Although you shouldn't use them everywhere, they can come in very useful in certain use cases and are thus another tool in your arsenal for creating good JavaScript code.

Index

A

addEventListener, 173, 182,
    184, 285
Animations, 303–305
Anonymous functions, 103–104
Application programming
    interfaces (API), 90
    advantages, 224
    canvas (*see* Canvas)
    description, 224
    HTTP, 226–240
    principles, 225
    REST, 225
    servers/web pages, 226
Array.prototype, 79, 80, 167, 168
Arrays, 43, 44, 94, 102, 110, 138,
    200, 253, 275, 276
    duplicates, 205
    forEach methods, 78
    last element, 45, 46
    length, 44, 45
    manipulation methods
        pop and shift, 47
        push and unshift, 47
        splice, 48, 49
    NodeList, 167, 169
    and objects, 76
    promises, 256

Arrow functions, 106, 107
Assignment operators, 26, 27
    template literals, 29
    variable concatenation, 27, 28
Asynchronicity, 248–257

B

Back-end JavaScript, 2, 9–12
Bitmap, 288
Block scoping
    logical statements, 36–38
    variables, 21, 22
Bubble phase, 180–185

C

Canvas
    additional contexts, 286, 287
    animations, 303–305
    API, 285
    arguments, 291–292
    DOM, 285
    drawing application, 299–303
    element, 288
    HTML, 286
    interactivity, 299–303
    in JavaScript, 286
Capture phase, 183–185

J. Simpson, *How JavaScript Works*, https://doi.org/10.1007/978-1-4842-9738-4

Printed in the United States
by Baker & Taylor Publisher Services